T0255275

Advanced Microservices

A Hands-on Approach to Microservice Infrastructure and Tooling

Thomas Hunter II

Apress®

Advanced Microservices: A Hands-on Approach to Microservice Infrastructure and Tooling

Thomas Hunter II
San Francisco, California, USA

IISBN-13 (pbk): 978-1-4842-2886-9   ISBN-13 (electronic): 978-1-4842-2887-6
DOI 10.1007/978-1-4842-2887-6

Library of Congress Control Number: 2017908960

Copyright © 2017 by Thomas Hunter II

This work is subject to copyright. All rights are reserved by the Publisher, whether the whole or part of the material is concerned, specifically the rights of translation, reprinting, reuse of illustrations, recitation, broadcasting, reproduction on microfilms or in any other physical way, and transmission or information storage and retrieval, electronic adaptation, computer software, or by similar or dissimilar methodology now known or hereafter developed.

Trademarked names, logos, and images may appear in this book. Rather than use a trademark symbol with every occurrence of a trademarked name, logo, or image we use the names, logos, and images only in an editorial fashion and to the benefit of the trademark owner, with no intention of infringement of the trademark.

The use in this publication of trade names, trademarks, service marks, and similar terms, even if they are not identified as such, is not to be taken as an expression of opinion as to whether or not they are subject to proprietary rights.

While the advice and information in this book are believed to be true and accurate at the date of publication, neither the authors nor the editors nor the publisher can accept any legal responsibility for any errors or omissions that may be made. The publisher makes no warranty, express or implied, with respect to the material contained herein.

Managing Director: Welmoed Spahr
Editorial Director: Todd Green
Acquisitions Editor: Louise Corrigan
Development Editor: James Markham
Technical Reviewers: Anthony Leontiev, Jonathan Kuperman, and John Sheehan
Coordinating Editor: Nancy Chen
Copy Editor: Kim Wimpsett

Distributed to the book trade worldwide by Springer Science+Business Media New York, 233 Spring Street, 6th Floor, New York, NY 10013. Phone 1-800-SPRINGER, fax (201) 348-4505, e-mail orders-ny@springer-sbm.com, or visit www.springeronline.com. Apress Media, LLC is a California LLC and the sole member (owner) is Springer Science + Business Media Finance Inc (SSBM Finance Inc). SSBM Finance Inc is a **Delaware** corporation.

For information on translations, please e-mail rights@apress.com, or visit www.apress.com/rights-permissions.

Apress titles may be purchased in bulk for academic, corporate, or promotional use. eBook versions and licenses are also available for most titles. For more information, reference our Print and eBook Bulk Sales web page at www.apress.com/bulk-sales.

Any source code or other supplementary material referenced by the author in this book is available to readers on GitHub via the book's product page, located at www.apress.com/9781484228869. For more detailed information, please visit www.apress.com/source-code.

Printed on acid-free paper

Contents at a Glance

Contents

About the Author

Thomas Hunter II is a principal software engineer at OpenTable where he maintains microservices, builds new ones as needed, and generates cURL requests for other teams to debug their services. His nights are occasionally spent giving talks at meetups and conferences. Thomas previously worked as an API architect for Barracuda Networks' Copy.com, a file-sharing and storage service, where his main concern was getting a nicely documented API into the hands of third-party developers.

About the Technical Reviewers

Anthony Leontiev is a senior architect at AltSchool, where he is a team lead on front and back-end development projects. He was previously a software engineer at Honest Buildings and has worn various hats at early to mid-stage startups. Anthony is building Asaak's mobile platform and automating the loan origination process. He is experienced with Python, Django, Ember, JavaScript, and React Native.

Jonathan Kuperman is a software engineer who is passionate about JavaScript, web performance, and accessibility. Jon worked as an engineer at Brave where he built a faster, safer, open source browser with Node.js and JavaScript. Before that he worked as a software engineer at Twitter, making the home timeline fast and accessible. He spends his free time speaking at conferences and giving workshops. He creates educational videos at Nodecasts.io for new developers. He is also the host of The Web Behind podcast, interviewing well-known developers on how they got their start in technology.

John Sheehan is an API fanatic with more than 15 years of experience working in a wide variety of IT and software development roles. As an early employee at Twilio, John led the developer evangelism program and worked as a product manager for Developer Experience. After Twilio, John was the platform lead at IFTTT working with API providers to create new channels. John is also the creator of Rest Sharp, API Digest, and API Jobs and is the cohost of Trac and Weather, an API and cloud podcast.

Preface

This book covers a breadth of knowledge for adopting and implementing redundant and highly available microservices within an organization. Preference is given to a stack built upon open source technologies. I use as few application code examples as possible to make this book language-agnostic. I also cover example network payloads and configuration files where applicable.

I explain some basic concepts such as how to design your application programming interface (API), how to keep track of other services consuming your API, and how to document your API. I cover how to deploy your API and let others know where your API can be found. I also explain how to keep your API alive and healthy using analytics, monitoring, and logging, and even have it alert you if it isn't healthy. I even discuss tools and methods for collaborating with other teams to keep the organization happy.

Intended Audience

Whether you already work for an organization that practices microservices or would like to convince your organization to start doing so, this book is for you. If the prior, it is my hope that this book will bring some understanding to your chaotic workday. If the latter, it is my hope to bring chaos to your orderly workday.

The ideal reader of this book is someone who has built several web sites and is comfortable working with a web language or framework, as well as having some intermediate knowledge such as how to read and write HTTP headers. Comfort with version control, especially with Git, is also beneficial.

Tools

Here are some tools that will help you not only while reading this book but also throughout your career as a microservice developer. I will cover them repeatedly throughout this book, so please install them.

- cURL (curl.haxx.se): Command-line Hypertext Transfer Protocol (HTTP) client

- jq (stedolan.github.io/jq): Command-line JavaScript Object Notation (JSON) transformer

- Postman (getpostman.com): Graphical HTTP client

Once you have cURL and jq installed, you will be able to run commands like this:

```
$ curl https://api.github.com/users/tlhunter | jq \
    "{name: .name, home: .location, where_to_spam: .email}"

{
  "name": "Thomas Hunter II",
  "home": "San Francisco, CA",
  "where_to_spam": "me@thomashunter.name"
}
```

CHAPTER 1

Introduction

Microservice Architecture is a pattern for implementing business logic within an organization using small, single-purpose services. This approach provides contrast to the traditional method of building monolithic services. There are various reasons to choose one approach instead of the other, and neither approach is absolutely better or worse than the other.

Why Use Microservices?

Let's look at the reasons you would want to choose to build smaller microservices instead of a monolith as well as the counter arguments.

Forced Separation of Concerns

In a monolith, you might be tempted to create global variables and share state between separate business logic modules, accidentally getting to the point of creating "spaghetti code." By separating business logic into different services, it becomes much harder to create tangled, complex code.

The argument against this point is that a team with a lot of self-control and skill can prevent themselves from tightly coupling two different modules of business logic within the same codebase.

Natural Team Ownership

By separating modules of logic into separate services, it becomes easy to draw the line and know which team owns which part of the project. With a microservice, a team will own the entire service. Teams can control everything about the service including deployment, monitoring, what language it is written in, and so on.

On the other hand, if a downstream service that your service relies on needs a change, you will most likely be blocked until the owner of the other service makes the change. If the other service is written in a different language or paradigm than what you're used to, there will be additional ramp-up time should you choose to contribute. Hunting down services and their owners can be difficult if the organization doesn't

© Thomas Hunter II 2017
T. Hunter II, *Advanced Microservices*, DOI 10.1007/978-1-4842-2887-6_1

maintain a directory of service ownership. Also, bugs existing in the codebase for another service will naturally be harder to find than bugs in the codebase of the service you normally work with.

Frequent Deployments

By owning a small part of the overall product (in other words, a single microservice), your team can choose when they want to deploy, perhaps even deploying several times a day (which is referred to as *continuous integration*). This allows for frequent testing of new features, A/B testing business decisions, and getting features into the hands of customers quicker.

One of the dangers of this is the risk of "moving fast and breaking things." Unless you're diligent about maintaining backward compatibility, you may release a change that breaks an upstream consumer of your service.

Heterogeneous Selection of Languages

By separating modules of business logic into their own microservices, each service can choose a different language or framework to be built in. This means that deep in the stack there can be a .NET service talking to Microsoft SQL, a Java service performing some heavy number crunching, and a Node.js service consuming both of them and generating Hypertext Markup Language (HTML) content for end consumers. There are certainly tools that are better suited for different problems.

Of course, every rose has its thorn. Some would argue that a company should specialize in a single language, employing only those who are proficient in said language. If the entire company practices Golang, then an employee could easily move from any one team to another without needing to learn a new language.

Organization Buy-In

For an organization there are a few standards that should be adopted by all teams to make the whole process run smoother. Try to get all of the key decision-makers into a single room and get everyone to agree on them; this will make everyone much happier.

Throughout this book there will be numerous Collaboration Tips. Heed these tips when you attempt to adopt standards within your organization.

Every service in your organization should have its own unique name. This name should be represented as lowercase letters, hyphens, and if necessary numbers.

> *There are only two hard things in computer science: cache invalidation and naming things.*
>
> —*Phil Karlton*

These names will be used programmatically and will come up multiple times throughout this book. Every log message should contain the service name. Analytic calls should all have the name as a prefix. Discovery lookups will use this name. Every outbound Hypertext Transfer Protocol (HTTP) request should have this name in the User-Agent header.

There should be a common place where any person in the organization can find more information about a project, and of course this information should be searchable using only this well-understood service name. I will cover this concept more in Chapter 8.

Separation of Concerns

How do you take a large, complex product and split it up into separate microservices? I'm glad you asked. There is no perfect way to slice up a product, and indeed if you were to ask ten experts to split up a product, you may get ten different answers. Let's look at an example organization and its products and see whether we can come up with a good approach.

At a very high level, Instagram is an app for sharing photos. Users can take a photo and share it, adding a location, a description, and tags. Users can "like" the photos of other users, follow users, and view a timeline of photos posted by users they follow. Users can also search for places or tags. To become a user, a person needs to register an account and confirm their e-mail, and all interactions require the user to be authenticated.

Nouns (Entities)

Now let's pull out a list of important nouns from the high-level description. This list may look like the following:

- *User*: A person using Instagram

- *Photo*: A photograph shared by a user

- *Location*: A real-world location

- *Tag*: A string to categorize photos

- *Timeline*: A collection of user photos over time

- *E-mail*: A message for confirming an account

This list can be used to define the high-level entities, which are types of data that you need to store somewhere. With this list you know that you need to have entities named User, Photo, Location, and Tag. E-mails are mostly ephemeral but still a type of entity. The last one, Timeline, despite being a noun, isn't so much an entity itself but rather a view into a list of Photo entities.

Verbs (Actions/Relationships)

Let's also look at some important verbs from the description.

- *Share*: Move a photo from a device to Instagram

- *Like*: A method for incrementing Internet karma

- *Follow*: Subscribe to a particular user's photos

- *Search*: Find photos based on criteria

- *Register*: Create a user

Each of these verbs can be thought of as an action, or a relationship, between one or two entities. To *share* is to create a photo. To *like* is to form a relation between a user and a photo. To *follow* is to relate a user and another user. To *search* is to list photos matching the specified criteria. To *register* is to create a user. And to *browse* a timeline is to list photos.

Typically you will want to have a separate service for each noun. Depending on the complexity of the verb, it may or may not warrant its own service. Figuring out how to separate these items becomes a science and an art. For apps such as Facebook, Twitter, and Instagram, the timeline is frequently the most important part of an application. Search is also an important component of many apps. Both timeline and search, which aggregate photos for a user, can become complex enough that they would warrant their own team and shouldn't live inside the Photo service.

Another common concern for separating data is how to retrieve user data versus how to authenticate a user. Authentication is something that needs to happen frequently and universally by many services. With most apps/services, every call will contain information about an authenticated user (such as a token). These need to be looked up quickly from many different services. However, the User entity, with a name and preferences and an e-mail address, probably needs to be accessed less frequently. So while user data and authentication are coupled, it is probably a good idea to keep them separate.

E-mail is another good item to separate. Perhaps when you first build this Instagram product, the only way to generate an e-mail is by creating an account. However, e-mail is the kind of thing that may one day be triggered by a myriad of events. Perhaps one day you'll want to e-mail a user after every like they receive. With these situations in mind, it is best to keep e-mail as its own service.

As a rule of thumb, you should be able to describe what a service does using a single sentence, and that sentence shouldn't contain the word *and*. For example, the User service shouldn't be described as "Manages users and e-mails account confirmation."

Example Microservice Breakdown

Here's a list of microservices you may arrive at for the Instagram example as well as some of the features of that service:

- *User*: Register account, close account

- *Authentication*: Generate token from username/password

- *Photo*: Store photos, resize photos, remove photos

- *Location*: Store locations, find location by latitude/longitude

- *Tag*: Store tags, create tags, remove tags

- *Timeline*: List photos

- *E-mail*: Send e-mail

- *Search*: List photos based on tags

The granularity an organization should choose for its services depends on the size of teams and complexity of each service. As an example, Instagram will need to resize each photo. Should this be part of the Photo service or is it worthy of its own service? If Instagram employs a team of hardcore engineers who know how to resize images as quickly as possible, then this function may warrant its own team.

Team Structure

> *Organizations which design systems ... are constrained to produce designs which are copies of the communication structures of these organizations.*
>
> —*Melvin Conway*

Now that I've described how a project can be separated into separate microservices, it may be worth mentioning how team organization should work. Teams and services will naturally form their own relationships. In the previous example, you may end up with a search/timeline/photo team.

However, some services might require so much sharing of knowledge that they should have combined ownership. You may find there's a single user team that owns the User, Authentication, and E-mail services.

Other microservices might be so static and simple that they simply don't require an entire dedicated team. In this case, you may end up with a photo attribute team that owns the Tag and Location microservices.

Of course, you'll want other types of teams as well. The previous examples have included "vertical" teams. These teams own, essentially, one part of the overall product. Each team runs pretty much autonomously and can choose whatever technologies they want to use. It's important to also develop "horizontal" teams that span all parts of the product. The most common horizontal team would be that of operations (ops). This team may be in charge of stuff that each vertical team doesn't want to be doing or re-creating over and over. This may include creating infrastructure, building services, managing build servers, and so on. A common design team is also important so that the user interface of each vertical is coherent.

Unfortunately, teams are not always easy to break apart. With Instagram, the company needs to create both iOS and Android applications. Should there be an Android team as well as an iOS team? Or, should each vertical have members contributing to the Android project (e.g., the timeline team has a member or two working on the Android timeline screen)? There is no perfect answer, and at the end of the day this question boils down to who wants to manage what.

Splitting a Monolith

Now that you've seen how you *should* organize a system of microservices, let's look at a few strategies for breaking up an existing monolith into smaller microservices.

One thing you shouldn't do is completely throw away an existing monolith and start from scratch using this cool new Microservice Architecture pattern you heard about. The amount of time required to rebuild a large service from scratch is about ten times longer than you think. During a rewrite, changes will happen in the original product, and the new one will start to diverge.

> ...[Netscape made] the single worst strategic mistake that any software company can make: They decided to rewrite the code from scratch.
>
> —*Joel Spolsky [1]*

Instead, what you want to do is slowly separate the monolith into smaller microservices, piece by piece. If you can, roll them out one at a time, ensuring each piece works in production and reproduces the necessary business logic before moving onto the next.

While moving small pieces from the monolith, try starting with the easier, "low-hanging fruit" first, such as sections of the application that aren't too tightly coupled. This can help build momentum; creating a new service can be difficult in an organization that is used to having a single type of service.

Going back to the Instagram example, perhaps you find that the user, authentication, and e-mail concerns are the easiest to extract. Afterward, you can move on to the tag and location features.

Any time you make a single query for data that crosses multiple concerns, such as getting data from a photo table based on an identifier from a user table, you'll need to separate it into multiple queries. Doing so will make the concerns easier to split when you're ready.

An example of this could be the natural tight coupling between users and authentication. With a monolithic service, you have a single database query look up a username and confirm the password while returning user data. After separating the concerns, you could have a single function for confirming a username and password, returning a user ID, and then another function to take a user ID and return user data.

Once you've chipped away at much of the monolith, retaining a single service with a few tightly coupled concerns, you should consider forking the codebase and running two instances of the monolith. Once the two are separated, you can slowly refactor and remove unused code. Some redundant code that still needs to exist in the two services can be extracted into a shareable module.

While splitting the fictional Instagram monolith, you may find that you're left with a single service that contains concerns regarding photos, the timeline, and search. These are naturally tightly coupled because they each deal intimately with photos and retrieving lists of photos. By duplicating the codebase into three pieces, you can then start to refactor.

As an example, the timeline and search codebases don't need any photo upload functionality, so you can remove it. You can then add an endpoint to the Photo service to accept a list of photo IDs for retrieval. Finally, you can create a shared module in the Timeline and Search services for specifying outbound requests to the Photo service.

Of course, splitting a monolith is not always this straightforward. You may find that after removing a few pieces either the rest is too tightly coupled or the remaining work becomes deprioritized. If this happens, all hope is not lost! By separating *some* of the monolith into microservices, you have made enough of a dent that future work is easier to perform.

Knowing when a service has gotten so large that it needs to be broken down into smaller services can be a difficult situation to spot. As you slowly add functionality into any service, it will approach monolith status. Splitting a large service isn't free, either. Essentially you need to ask yourself whether a project has become so large that either it is becoming difficult to maintain or it's violating the *and* description test mentioned earlier. Once you spot this type of situation, try to prioritize the work to split the service.

Terminology

Before getting too deep into things, let's look at some terms used throughout the book as well as their definitions. Some of them are synonymous, and some terms refer to a subset of other terms.

- *Machine*: Traditionally the word *machine* referred to a physical computer, though now it can refer to virtual machines as well. A physical machine is hardware that runs an operating system (OS) and has processing power and memory available.

- *Virtual machine*: A virtual machine (VM) is an operating system running somewhere on a physical machine. It will have processing power and memory allocated to it from the physical machine on which it resides. Many VMs can exist on one physical machine; they can even be nested.

- *Container*: A container is a special type of isolation that exists inside an OS. Whereas a machine needs to have its own OS, a container can access the OS of the machine it resides on, removing the need for redundant OSs required by VMs.

- *Host*: A host is a machine that is accessible on a network. It will have an Internet Protocol (IP) address associated with it and potentially a hostname as well.

- *Service*: A service is a project or codebase that is intended to perform long-running functionality.

- *Microservice*: A microservice is a type of specially built service, performing as few functions as possible.

- *Instance*: An instance is a running copy of a service. There can be one or many instances of a service running at once. Each instance can have its own configuration settings.

- *Node*: A node is an instance that has access to and communicates via a network. I typically only refer to instances as nodes in the context of discussing their role in a network.

- *Application*: An application is a collection of similarly configured instances. Instances are ephemeral but still contribute to the same application.

- *Environment*: An environment represents a collection of applications configured to communicate with other applications in the same environment.

- *Consumer*: A consumer is a node that requests data from a provider. A node can be both a consumer and a provider.

- *Client*: The term *client* is synonymous with *consumer*. A device outside of the organization consuming data is more likely to be called a client than a consumer.

- *Provider*: A provider is a node that provides a resource or other functionality over the network for other nodes to consume.

- *Server*: A server is an ambiguous term. Traditionally it referred to a physical machine; however, it can also refer to a service (e.g., a web server can mean the physical server hardware or software such as Nginx). Try to always use *service* to refer to software.

Networking Basics

Let's discuss some basic networking concepts that relate to building services exposed over a network. I'll briefly explain some concepts you've probably heard of but might not be too familiar with such as hostnames, IP addresses, network interfaces, ports, and protocols.

Knowing this basic network information will help with later chapters of the book. There's a good chance you're already familiar with these concepts, in which case feel free to skip this section entirely.

Hostnames and IP Addresses

IP addresses (e.g., 45.79.98.236) are how you refer to devices on networks. They can be either public, which means they can be accessed anywhere on the Internet, or private, meaning they're accessible only when on the same network. A networking device can include a computer capable of responding to requests. Sometimes they are more complex such as routers that take requests and forward them to other networking devices, though I won't be covering routers here.

Hostnames (e.g., `api.radar.chat`) are convenient ways to point to an IP address. A hostname can potentially resolve to one of multiple potential IP addresses. The translation between hostname to IP address is a complex topic and includes technology such as the Domain Name System (DNS), which performs these lookups. At a lower level, these lookups can be set manually using a hosts file. Listing 1-1 shows the default locations for hosts files.

Listing 1-1. Default Hosts File Locations

```
*nix:    /etc/hosts
Windows: c:\Windows\System32\Drivers\etc\hosts
```

Network Interfaces

Networking interfaces represent a gateway between a server and the outside world. Typically each physical networking device on a computer will have an associated interface (assuming it works and has a driver).

There are also virtual and otherwise special interfaces available on a machine. These don't necessarily connect the server externally but can be used for other special kinds of communications. An example of a virtual interface is the default Docker `docker0` interface.

Network interfaces have IP addresses associated with them. These IP addresses are used for routing messages from one machine's interface to another interface across a network.

To view a list of interfaces available on your Linux or macOS computer, run the command $ `ifconfig` (if you're using Windows, run $ `ipconfig`). You should see a list of interfaces, each with names and associated IP addresses.

Listing 1-2 contains a truncated list from the output on my machine.

Listing 1-2. Example Network Interfaces

```
wlan0     Link encap:Ethernet   HWaddr 18:5e:0f:a5:32:ff
          inet addr:10.0.0.10

docker0   Link encap:Ethernet   HWaddr 02:42:8f:c3:27:e9
          inet addr:172.17.0.1

lo        Link encap:Local Loopback
          inet addr:127.0.0.1
```

There are three interfaces, explained here:

- `wlan0`: The first interface is a physical one. In particular, it is the interface associated with the wireless card in my machine. On your machine, you may see a device with a different name, maybe `eth0`. The IP address of this interface is `10.0.0.10`. This is the IP address of the computer on my personal network.

- docker0: This is a virtual interface used by Docker. It the default method Docker uses for bridging connections between containers and the rest of the world. You'll look at this in more depth in Chapter 3.

- lo: This is a special interface representing the "local loopback." It is used to represent the current machine. Chances are you've run some sort of web server on your computer in the past and had to access it by visiting http://localhost. Requests to the hostname localhost translate into 127.0.0.1, and this is configured in your hosts file.

There is another important special IP address you should know about, which is 0.0.0.0. This address represents all interfaces on a machine.

When networking software on a machine (a service running on a server) is listening for requests, it needs to bind to a particular interface. If it chooses to bind on a physical interface, it will receive only those requests sent over that interface. By binding to a virtual interface, it will receive only those requests made through that virtual networking device.

When it binds to localhost/127.0.0.1, it will receive only those requests made from inside the current machine. This is useful in situations where a database should receive only local connections (especially tools that are by default insecure such as Redis and MongoDB). It's also good for running local test versions of software.

When it binds to 0.0.0.0, it will receive connections regardless of the interface a request comes in on. Since keeping track of the IP addresses of each interface could be painful, it's a great way to ensure your application is getting requests from everywhere.

Ports

When making requests (as well as listening for requests), you can't simply make use of an IP address but must also specify a port. Port numbers are integers ranging from 1 to 65,535. When representing a specific combination of either a hostname or an IP address with a port number, you concatenate the value using a colon as a separator, as shown in Listing 1-3.

Listing 1-3. Port Syntax

```
8.8.4.4:53
thomashunter.name:80
```

Some ports are *well-known*, meaning that it's widely understood what their purpose is [2]. Some examples of this include HTTP using 80 and SSH using 22. When ports are well-known, it is usually sufficient to omit them when making requests using client software. The most common example of this is when you request a web site, you can enter example.com instead of entering the more verbose example.com:80.

High-level ports, specifically those numbered from 49,152 to 65,535, are known as *ephemeral ports* and will never be well-known. It's a first-come, first-serve situation when services can grab whichever one is available and listen for requests.

Protocols

There are two important basic protocols that I will cover here. The simpler one is called User Datagram Protocol (UDP), and the more complex is called Transmission Control Protocol (TCP). These are often used as building blocks for building higher-level protocols, such as HTTP, which is based on TCP.

The smallest unit of data that you can send over a network is a packet. These packets contain information used to find a destination as well as data intended to be shared. A single HTTP request can span many different TCP packets, though a small HTTP request could be represented in a single packet.

TCP includes a system for "guaranteeing" the delivery of packets over a network. If a packet is lost, it will be retransmitted. Packets will be properly ordered when being passed to listening software. This additional layer of guarantees comes with some network overhead, however, because you need to perform handshakes and an acknowledgment of packet receipt.

UDP does not include any of these guarantees. Packets that are sent may never be received, and software will never know whether a packet is received unless the software has its own message delivery guarantee system on top. This is useful for transmitting data that can be lost and needs to be delivered quickly such as with character movement in computer games or when transmitting high volumes of log data.

Typically the syntax for specifying a protocol is a superset of the syntax used for specifying host:port combinations. The port number can typically be omitted when the default well-known port for the protocol is used. You can see an example of this in Listing 1-4.

Listing 1-4. Protocol Syntax

```
https://thomashunter.name:443
https://thomashunter.name
```

CHAPTER 2

▓ ▓ ▓

HTTP API Design

An application programming interface (API) represents a contract between the data and business logic provided by your service and the consumers who want to interact with this data. Breaking this contract will result in angry e-mails from developers and anguished users with broken apps. Designing an externally facing and hard-to-use API will result in few or no third-party developers using it. Similarly, if you do this with an internal API, then people will talk about you behind your back.

On the other hand, building a great external API and adhering to this contract will result in substantially more third-party developers and can elevate your service from a closed-source product to an open platform. Building a great internal API might even result in your co-workers buying you a beer.

Data Design and Abstraction

Designing a friendly Hypertext Transfer Protocol (HTTP) API means abstracting the intricate business logic and data your service uses into the four basic CRUD operations (create, read, update, delete). Your application may perform many complex actions behind the scenes such as sending a text message or resizing an image or moving a file, but if you do enough planning and abstraction, everything can be represented as CRUD.

Architecting your API begins earlier than you may think; first you need to decide how your data will be stored and how your service/application functions. If you're practicing API-First Development, this is all part of the process [3]. However, if you're bolting an API onto an existing project, you will have more abstraction to take care of.

In an idealized, overly simple service, a collection can represent a database table, and a resource can represent a row within that table. As real-world practice will show, this is rarely the case, especially if the existing data design is overly complex. It is important that you don't overwhelm third-party developers with complex application data; otherwise, they won't want to use your API.

There will be parts of your service that you *should not* expose via an API at all. A common example is that many APIs will not allow consumers to create or delete user accounts or data shared between many accounts.

Sometimes multiple tables will be represented as a single resource (such as a JOIN statement). You might even find that one table could be represented as multiple resources (although you may have made some poor database design decisions if this is the case).

© Thomas Hunter II 2017
T. Hunter II, *Advanced Microservices*, DOI 10.1007/978-1-4842-2887-6_2

Examples of Abstraction

For both of these examples of abstraction, I'll use the same fictional service. This service sends messages to different users, and messages can be sent as either a text message or an e-mail. The chosen method depends on the preference of the particular user.

Don't worry too much about the technical parts of the examples because I'll cover them with more detail throughout this chapter. For now just think of them as simple function calls with inputs and outputs.

Good Abstraction

Listing 2-1 shows an example of a clean and simple approach for sending a notification.

Listing 2-1. Creating a Notification

```
POST /notifications

{
  "user_id": "12",
  "message": "Hello World"
}

{
  "id": "1000",
  "user_id": "12",
  "message": "Hello World",
  "medium": "email",
  "created": "2013-01-06T21:02:00Z"
}
```

In this example, you use a single endpoint for sending a notification to a user. The first JavaScript Object Notation (JSON) document is the request, and the second is the response. This endpoint is called notifications, and the consumer interacts by creating new notification resources. When the consumer wants to notify a user, it is conceptually creating a new notification resource, thereby abstracting the concept of performing an action with creating an object.

An important concept of this example is that the business logic of determining which method of contacting a user is abstracted away from the consumer entirely, which is why there is no endpoint for getting the user's notification preference. In the background, the service is taking the appropriate action and hiding it from the consumer.

In the example response in Listing 2-1, you can see a medium attribute that represents the method of notifying the user but that can be omitted depending on whether your consumers need to know this information (perhaps their application has a dashboard that mentions the last time a text/e-mail was sent and the verbiage should be correct or perhaps this would be a security leak of user preference).

Bad Abstraction

Listing 2-2 includes numerous shortcomings and is an easy approach to take by the novice HTTP API architect.

Listing 2-2. Getting User Preference

```
GET /get_user_preferences/12

{
  "notification_preference": 1
}
```

This first API endpoint is called `get_user_preferences` and is called by passing in the ID of the user whose preference you are looking up (shown here as 12). The name of an endpoint should be a simple noun (or compound nouns). It should not include the action (verb) being performed (in this case get). The reason you should use a simple noun is because this removes ambiguity and tells the consumer what the ID represents. Does 12 represent user 12? Or perhaps it represents some user preference concept that might not correlate one to one to a user object?

Another problem with this example is the response contains the integer 1. Internally to this fictional service there are some constants where 1 refers to sending a text and 2 refers to sending an e-mail. Even if these values are disclosed in the API documentation, a third-party developer is not going to remember what they represent. Each time they look up what the values mean, they are losing productivity. On the flip side, if this service is consumed only internally and a numeric identifier is widely understood, it may then become acceptable.

Yet another problem is that there's an API endpoint dedicated specifically to getting a user preference. In general, you should strive to reduce the number of endpoints in your API, focusing on making each one serve the consumer better. Data like this could have been merged with another endpoint for getting a user object, for example.

These second and third endpoints (assuming {medium} can represent email or text), shown in Listing 2-3, have the same problem as the previous endpoint wherein the action is part of the URL (in this case send). These endpoints don't represent data, as the previous one did; they specifically represent an action. Building APIs with these actionable endpoints is a common mistake among developers intending to build a RESTful API.

Listing 2-3. Sending a Text or E-mail (Two Endpoints)

```
POST /users/12/send_{medium}

{
  "message": "Hello World",
  "sent": "2013-01-06T21:02:00Z"
}
```

Another issue with this example is that the business logic for determining which method of notification to use is left for the consumer to decide! Sure, the consumer can make a request to get the user's preference, but what if the developer intentionally ignores the value? Or suppose the consumer caches the preference and it becomes outdated. Either way, users are bound to get notified in a manner they didn't choose.

Whenever you find yourself creating two endpoints with the same request inputs and response outputs, there may be a problem with abstraction, and the two endpoints may be better off combined into one.

Finally, there is no way to look up previous instances of notifications that have been sent to a user. While another endpoint could have been created for looking up notification logs, it would likely be ad hoc or inconsistent with existing endpoints.

Real-World Examples

Let's look at some real-world examples of how popular APIs do their data abstraction.

GitHub: An Ideal Example

The current GitHub v3 API is a beautiful example of a properly abstracted HTTP API [4]. Each of the popular HTTP verbs is leveraged where applicable. Endpoints don't have verbs in the name. Interacting with an endpoint feels much like you are working with a representation of an object instead of performing actions.

One such exemplary endpoint is `GET /repos/{user_id}/{repo_id}/notifications`. This is obviously the endpoint used for getting a list of notifications of a particular repository. The `{user_id}/ {repo_id}` convention for referring to a repository is one understood by most users of GitHub (repository names aren't globally unique; they are unique to a particular user). The only thing that could be improved may be to not shorten `repositories` to `repos` and `organizations` to `orgs` in the names of endpoints, although `repo` is well understood by the GitHub community.

Twitter: A Flawed Example

The current Twitter v1.1 API has some shortcomings with its data and business-logic abstraction as far as being an HTTP API is concerned [5]. The API only makes use of the GET and POST methods for interacting with data. Because of this shortcoming, most endpoint names are a pair of noun and verbs.

One such example is `POST /statuses/destroy/{status_id}`, which is used for deleting a status. A cleaner version of this endpoint would be `DELETE /statuses/{status_id}`. Also worth noting is the differentiation of `POST /statuses/update_with_media` and `POST /statuses/update`. Both of these endpoints are used for creating a new tweet; however, the prior allows for the attachment of media. These two endpoints should be combined into a single `POST /statuses` with the media-related attributes being optional.

These endpoints are also an example of bad nomenclature. Users of Twitter don't think of using the service as updating their status; they think of it as *tweeting*. This is something that may have changed throughout the lifetime of the service and if so would be a good candidate to rename between API versions. The collection used by the aforementioned endpoints would therefore be better named as `tweets`.

Anatomy of an HTTP Message

Let's examine some raw HTTP messages since HTTP is the protocol you're using to build your API. It's surprising how many developers who have been building web sites for years don't know what an HTTP message looks like! When the consumer sends a request to the server, it provides Request-Line data and a set of key/value pairs called *headers*. For POST, PUT, and PATCH requests, it also provides two newlines and then the request body. All this information is sent in the same HTTP request (although this request can be broken up into multiple TCP packets if the message is large enough). Listing 2-4 shows an example of a complete HTTP request.

Listing 2-4. HTTP Request

```
POST /v1/animal HTTP/1.1
Host: api.example.org
Accept: application/json
Content-Type: application/json
Content-Length: 24

{
  "name": "Gir",
  "animal_type": "12"
}
```

The server then replies in a similar format, first with Status-Line data and headers and typically two newlines followed by a body (the body is technically optional, as you'll find out later). HTTP/1.1 is very much a request/response protocol; there is no *push* support (the server does not send data to the consumer unprovoked). To do that, you would need to use a different protocol such as WebSockets. Listing 2-5 shows an example of a complete HTTP response.

Listing 2-5. HTTP Response

```
HTTP/1.1 200 OK
Date: Wed, 18 Dec 2013 06:08:22 GMT
Content-Type: application/json
Access-Control-Max-Age: 1728000
Cache-Control: no-cache

{
  "id": "12",
  "created": "2013-12-18T06:08:22Z",
  "modified": null,
  "name": "Gir",
  "animal_type": "12"
}
```

Debugging HTTP Traffic

Postman is an excellent tool for interacting with an HTTP API. As shown in Figure 2-1, Postman provides a powerful yet easy-to-use interface for building API requests as well as debugging the content of API responses. It also provides many advanced features regarding authentication (which I'll cover in later chapters).

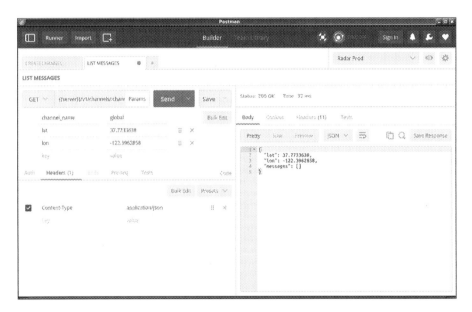

Figure 2-1. *Postman*

While designing and debugging your API, you will sometimes need to debug packets at a lower level than HTTP. A powerful tool for doing this is Wireshark. You will also want to use a web framework and server, which allows you to read and change as many headers as possible.

Figure 2-2 shows an example of a complex HTTP request from a form submission on a web site. Notice all the data sent back and forth via HTTP headers. The headers passed around by browsers and web servers are often noisier and more chaotic than what an API consumer and server will send.

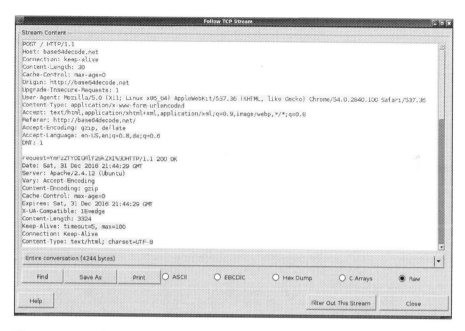

Figure 2-2. *Wireshark*

API Entrypoint

The root location of your API is important, believe it or not. When a third-party developer (aka *code archaeologist*) inherits a project using your API and needs to build new features, they may not know about your service at all. Perhaps all they know is a list of URLs that the consumer communicates with. It's important that the root entry point into your API is as simple as possible because a long complex URL will appear daunting and can turn developers away.

Choosing an Entrypoint for a Public API

Here are two common entrypoints that developers use when building an API:

- `https://api.example.com/*` (preferred)

- `https://example.com/api/*` (security implications)

First notice the `https` prefix. If API communication is sent unencrypted over the Internet, then any third party along the way is able to eavesdrop. This could include reading sensitive API data and, depending on the chosen authentication method, could allow third parties to make requests on behalf of the user. However, if this API is exposed only internally in a single-tenant environment, you may *not* want to use HTTPS. The minor security gain is probably not worth the overhead. Since the inception of Let's Encrypt, a service to easily create and maintain SSL/TLS certificates for free, there is no valid excuse to not encrypt a public API.

If your application is huge or you anticipate it becoming huge, putting the API on a dedicated subdomain (in this case api) is a must. This will allow for more scalability options in the future. It can also be useful for controlling what cookie data can be shared between the content web site and the API.

If you anticipate your API will never become large, if you want to build a simple application (e.g., you want to host the web site *and* API from the same framework), or if your API is entirely anonymous or read-only, placing your API beneath a URL segment at the root of the domain (e.g., /api/) will also work though it is still not a great idea. More considerations will need to be made regarding security, and more potential vulnerabilities can arise. For example, if a cross-site scripting (XSS) vulnerability is discovered on the main web site, credentials that might not otherwise be exposed can now be hijacked by a devious third party.

Do not use a different top-level domain (TLD) for hosting your API than for hosting your web site. This may sound tempting because your main domain could be example.com and your API and developer documentation could be entirely located on the trendy example.io. However, there is no intrinsic relationship between these two domains because an adversary could have purchased example.io, posing as a legitimate counterpart to example.com. Also, the *code archaeologist* might have knowledge of only one domain and not the other. Finally, if you *do* want to share cookies between the two domains (e.g., an authenticated user on example.com can be automatically logged into the developer site), it cannot be done as easily with two separate TLDs than with a subdomain or even a subdirectory.

Content Located at the Root

It's beneficial to consumers to have content at the root of your API. Accessing the root of GitHub's API returns a listing of endpoints. Personally I'm a fan of having the root URL give information that a lost developer would find useful such as how to get to the developer documentation.

Listing 2-6 contains a truncated list of the content provided by the GitHub API entrypoint.

Listing 2-6. GitHub API Entrypoint

```
{
  "current_user_url": "https://api.github.com/user",
  "authorizations_url":
    "https://api.github.com/authorizations",
  "emails_url": "https://api.github.com/user/emails",
  "starred_url":
    "https://api.github.com/user/starred{/owner}{/repo}",
  ...
}
```

The syntax used to describe these URLs is called a *URI template* and is a human-readable and machine-parsable standard for describing URLs. This is a great way to convey URLs both in your API documentation and in the API responses themselves.

This notation is used throughout the book to show when string substitutions can occur. According to RFC 6570 [6], "A URI Template is a compact sequence of characters for describing a range of Uniform Resource Identifiers through variable expansion."

Information about the currently authenticated user can also be placed in the root of the API. For example, either the user ID or the URL to the user would make a great candidate. If you take a similar approach to what GitHub does, one of the keys could be current_user, and the value could be a URL to the users endpoint prepopulated with the current user's user_id.

It may be tempting to create an endpoint called /user or /users/me for accessing information about the current user, but these would contradict the existing URL patterns the rest of the API adheres to.

API Requests

There is a myriad of data that can be provided to your service when a consumer makes a request using HTTP. Let's take a look at this data and the correct ways to handle it.

HTTP Methods

You probably already know about GET and POST requests. These are the two most commonly used requests when a web browser accesses web pages and interacts with data. There are, however, four and a half HTTP methods that you need to know about when building an HTTP API. I say "and a half" because the PATCH method is similar to the PUT method and the functionality of the two are often combined by many APIs into just PUT.

You've likely heard of the phrase CRUD when referring to the seemingly boilerplate code many web developers need to write when interacting with a database. Some web frameworks will even generate CRUD *scaffolding* for the developer as a result of running a terminal command. CRUD stands for create, read, update, and delete, and it can be used for handling all data entry.

Here is a list of HTTP methods as well as which CRUD operation they represent. The correlated SQL command is also provided, assuming your service were to represent an extremely simple database.

- POST (create)

    - Creates a new resource on the server

    - Corresponds to a SQL INSERT command

    - Not considered *idempotent* because multiple requests will create duplicate resources

- GET (read)

    - Retrieves a specific resource from the server

    - Retrieves a collection of resources from the server

    - Considered *safe*, meaning this request should not alter the server state

21

- Considered *idempotent* , meaning duplicate subsequent requests should be free from side effects

- Corresponds to a SQL SELECT command

- PUT (update)

    - Updates a resource on the server

    - Provides the entire resource

    - Considered *idempotent* , meaning duplicate subsequent requests should be free from side effects

    - Corresponds to a SQL UPDATE command, providing null values for missing columns

- PATCH (update)

    - Updates a resource on the server

    - Provides only changed attributes

    - Corresponds to a SQL UPDATE command, specifying only columns being updated

- DELETE (delete)

    - Destroys a resource on the server

    - Considered *idempotent* , meaning duplicate subsequent requests should be from side effects

    - Corresponds to a SQL DELETE command

Here are two lesser-known HTTP methods. While it isn't always necessary that they be implemented in your API, in some situations (such as APIs accessed via web browser from a different domain) their inclusion is mandatory.

- HEAD

    - Retrieves metadata about a resource (just the headers)

    - Example: a hash of the data or when it was last updated

    - Considered *safe*, meaning this request should not alter server state

    - Considered *idempotent*, meaning duplicate subsequent requests should be free from side effects

- OPTIONS

    - Retrieves information about what the consumer can do with the resource

    - Modern browsers precede all cross-origin resource sharing requests with an OPTIONS request

    – Considered *safe*, meaning this request should not alter server state

    – Considered *idempotent* , meaning duplicate subsequent requests should be free from side effects

By using the HTTP methods and not using actionable verbs within the URL itself, a simple and consistent interface is presented to the developer. Instead of wondering which verbs apply to which nouns ("Do I send or `mail` an *e-mail*? Do I remove or `fire` an *employee*?"), an unambiguous and consistent convention is provided.

Typically GET requests can and often will be cached. Browsers will aggressively cache GET requests (depending on expiration headers) and go as far as to alert the user if they attempt to POST data for a second time. A HEAD request is basically a GET without the response body and can be cached as well.

If you plan on allowing JavaScript consumers running within web browsers that make requests from different domains, the OPTIONS method must be supported. There is a feature called *cross-origin resource sharing* (CORS), which makes use of the OPTIONS header [7]. Basically it provides a set of request and response headers for defining which domains can access data and which HTTP methods they can utilize.

URL Endpoints

An endpoint is a URL within your API that provides a method to interact with a single resource or a collection of resources. A typical HTTP API will use a plural naming convention for collections.

Top-Level Collections

Pretend that you're building a fictional API to represent several different zoos. Each contains many animals (with an animal belonging to exactly one zoo) as well as employees (who can work at multiple zoos). You also want to keep track of the species of each animal. Figure 2-3 represents this relationship.

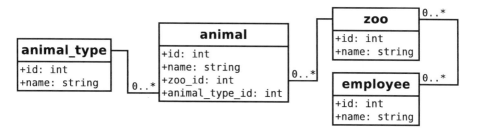

Figure 2-3. *Relationships*

Given this data and these relationships, you might have the following endpoints:

- `https://api.example.com/v1/zoos`
- `https://api.example.com/v1/animals`

- `https://api.example.com/v1/animal_types`

- `https://api.example.com/v1/employees`

Each piece of data separated by a slash is a URL segment. Try to keep the number of segments per endpoint as short as possible.

Specific Endpoints

While conveying what each endpoint does, you'll want to list valid HTTP method and endpoint combinations. For example, here's a list of actions that you can perform with your fictional zoo-keeping API. Notice you precede each endpoint with the HTTP method. This is a common notation and is similar to the one used within an HTTP request status line.

- `GET /v1/zoos`: List all zoos (perhaps just ID and name)

- `POST /v1/zoos`: Create a new zoo

- `GET /v1/zoos/{zoo_id}`: Get entire zoo resource

- `PUT /v1/zoos/{zoo_id}`: Update zoo (entire resource)

- `PATCH /v1/zoos/{zoo_id}`: Update zoo (partial resource)

- `DELETE /v1/zoos/{zoo_id}`: Delete zoo

- `GET /v1/zoos/{zoo_id}/animals`: List animals (ID and name) at this zoo

- `GET /v1/animals`: List all animals (ID and name)

- `POST /v1/animals`: Create new animal

- `GET /v1/animals/{animal_id}`: Get animal

- `PUT /v1/animals/{animal_id}`: Update animal (entire resource)

- `PATCH /v1/animals/{animal_id}`: Update animal (partial resource)

- `GET /v1/animal_types`: List all animal types (ID and name)

- `GET /v1/animal_types/{animaltype_id}`: Get entire animal type resource

- `GET /v1/employees`: List all employees

- `GET /v1/employees/{employee_id}`: Get specific employee

- `GET /v1/zoos/{zoo_id}/employees`: List employees at this zoo

- `POST /v1/employees`: Create new employee

- `POST /v1/zoos/{zoo_id}/employees`: Hire an employee for zoo

- `DELETE /v1/zoos/{zoo_id}/employees/{employee_id}`: Fire employee from zoo

The entrypoint prefix has been omitted in the previous examples for brevity. While this can be fine during informal communication (or books with limited page width), your actual API documentation would be better suited displaying the full URL to each endpoint. If your API is internal and has dynamic hostnames, then the host should be omitted.

Notice how the relationships between data are conveyed, such as the many-to-many relationships between employees and zoos. By adding an additional URL segment, you can perform relationship interactions. Of course, there is no HTTP verb like *fire* for firing an employee, but by performing a DELETE on an employee located within a zoo, you're able to achieve the same goal.

Also notice how this listing of endpoints doesn't include every possible method-to-resource combination. For example, a consumer is unable to POST or DELETE to the `animal_types` endpoints. In this fictional situation, only administrators would be able to add new `animal_types` using some mechanism outside of the API. Even for trusted internal APIs, exposing every possible combination might not be desirable.

There's nothing wrong with not supporting every method-to-resource combination because every conceptual data manipulation your service offers doesn't necessarily need to be exposed via an API. Just keep in mind developers may wonder why certain features aren't available, and they may even attempt to use an undocumented endpoint (such as deleting an `animal_type`). Know that if the functionality isn't documented, an industrious developer may still discover a hidden feature by brute force. Be intentional with the endpoints you implement and mindful of security.

Filtering Resources

When a consumer makes a GET request for a collection, provide them with a list of every resource matching the requested criteria even though the list could be quite large. Do your best to minimize arbitrary limitations imposed on consumers because these limits make it harder for a third-party developer to grok the API. If they request a collection and iterate over the results, never seeing more than 100 items, it is now their mission to determine where this limit is imposed. Is their object-relational mapping (ORM) buggy and limiting items to 100? Is the network chopping up large responses?

Do offer the ability for a consumer to specify some sort of filtering/limitation of the results. The most important reason for this, as far as the consumer is concerned, is that the network payload is minimal and the consumer receives results as soon as possible. Another reason for this is the consumer may be lazy and want the server to perform filtering and pagination. The not-so-important reason from the consumer's perspective, yet a great benefit for the server, is that response generation will require less CPU effort.

Since these are GET requests on collections, filters should be passed via URL parameters. Here are some examples of the types of filtering you could conceivably add to your API and, if your API were a simple representation of a relational database, the correlating SQL clause:

- `?limit=10&offset=20`: Pagination and offsetting of results (`LIMIT 20, 10`)

- `?animal_type_id=1`: Filter records that match the following condition (`WHERE animal_type_id = 1`)

- `?sort attribute=name,asc`: Sort the results based on the specified attributes (`ORDER BY name ASC`)

Some filtering can be redundant with other endpoints. In the endpoints section, you had a GET /zoo/{zoo_id}/animals endpoint. This would be the same thing as GET /animals?zoo_id={zoo_id}. Dedicated endpoints will make API consumption easier for developers. This is especially true with requests you anticipate will be made frequently. In your documentation, mention this redundancy so that developers aren't left wondering what the differences are.

White-Listing Attributes

Oftentimes when a consumer is making a GET request to a specific resource or collection, they do not need all attributes belonging to the resource (or resources). Having so much data could become a network bottleneck as well. Responding with less data can help reduce server overhead. For example, it may prevent an unnecessary database JOIN.

Again, since we're dealing with GET requests, you'll want to accept a URL parameter for white-listing attributes. In theory, black-listing could work as well, but as new attributes appear in resources (since additions are backward compatible), the consumer ends up receiving data it doesn't want.

The parameter name you choose isn't too important. It could be filter or the overly verbose attribute_whitelist. Consistency between all endpoints is what is most important.

The SQL queries in these examples are over-simplification of what could be generated if your API represented a simple relational database application.

Filtered Request

In this example, the consumer has requested a filtered list of attributes pertaining to a user. You can see the user's request in Listing 2-7, the corresponding SQL query in Listing 2-8, and the response in Listing 2-9.

Listing 2-7. Request URL

```
GET http://api.example.org/user/12?whitelist=id,name,email
```

Listing 2-8. Resulting SQL Query

```
SELECT id, name, email FROM user WHERE user.id = 12;
```

Listing 2-9. Response Body

```
{
  "id": "12",
  "name": "Thomas Hunter II",
  "email": "me@thomashunter.name"
}
```

Unfiltered Request

In this example request, the default representation of a user resource includes data from two database tables joined together. One of the tables is a user table, and another table contains some textual data related to a user called user_desc. Again, you can see the user's request in Listing 2-10, the corresponding SQL query in Listing 2-11, and the response in Listing 2-12.

Listing 2-10. Request URL

```
GET http://api.example.org/user/12
```

Listing 2-11. Resulting SQL Query

```
SELECT * FROM user LEFT JOIN user_desc ON
    user.id = user_desc.id WHERE user.id = 12;
```

Listing 2-12. Response Body

```
{
  "id": "12",
  "name": "Thomas Hunter II",
  "age": 27,
  "email": "me@thomashunter.name",
  "description": "Blah blah blah blah blah."
}
```

Requesting Arrays via URL Parameters

One source of ambiguity with simple GET requests is how a consumer makes a request for arrays of data using URL parameters. The HTTP specification doesn't mention how to handle this situation. Let's look at a few different methods and explore the pros and cons of each.

One such use for specifying an array in a request is to get multiple resources from a provider using a single HTTP request (making 100 parallel requests to a server instead of 1 asking for 100 records will severely tax the service). While getting multiple records in a single URL violates RESTful practices, it is sometimes the only solution to getting a list of data in a performant manner.

> **Collaboration Tip**: It doesn't matter so much *which* method you choose to use within an organization as much as it matters *that you do* choose one to standardize on. Generating different formats within a single node and remembering which providers expect which format is painful.

Repeat Parameters

Listing 2-13 shows the most common format I've encountered for requesting an array of items using query parameters.

Listing 2-13. Array of Parameters Repeating

```
?resourceid=1&resourceid=2&resourceid=3
```

This method is simple to reason about and is probably the most "correct" choice you'll see. Multiple items are simply repeated as normal key/value pairs. This is usually the default output from query string–generating libraries when provided an array to serialize.

A shortcoming of this approach is the verbosity. If the parameter name is long, then additional bytes of data need to be sent over the wire.

Bracket Notation

Listing 2-14 shows the default behavior in PHP for providing arrays in a request, and many query string libraries can output this format or parse it. There is also no ambiguity as to a singular item being read as a string versus an array.

Listing 2-14. Array of Parameters with Brackets

```
?resourceid[]=1&resourceid[]=2&resourceid[]=3
```

Unfortunately, this is even more verbose than the previous approach!

Comma Separated

The approach in Listing 2-15 is the least common. I haven't seen it officially supported in any query string serialization/deserialization libraries, and it will probably require you to write your own application code to split the query string on commas.

Listing 2-15. Array of Parameters Using Commas

```
?resourceid=1,2,3
```

The best thing about this approach is that it is the tersest, with items being separated by a single byte.

Body Formats

A common method for APIs to receive data from third parties is to accept a JSON document as the body. Assuming your API provides data to third parties in the form of JSON, those same third parties should also be able to produce JSON documents.

There are two primary methods a web browser will use when sending data to a web server. If you're using a popular web language/framework for building an API such as PHP or Express.js or Ruby on Rails, then you're already used to consuming data using these two methods. Web servers (such as Apache or Nginx) abstract the differences of these two methods and will provide your programming language with one easy method to consume data. The two methods are called *multipart form data* (required for file uploads) and *URL form encoded* (most forms use the latter method).

JSON

The JSON document used for the request should be similar to the JSON document used for the response, such as the one in Listing 2-16. JSON can specify the type of data (e.g., integers, strings, Booleans) while also allowing for hierarchal relationships of data. String data needs to be escaped (e.g., a quote, ", becomes prefixed with a backslash, \"), but this is usually done automatically by a serializer.

Listing 2-16. JSON Request Body Format

```
POST /v1/animal HTTP/1.1
Host: api.example.org
Accept: application/json
Content-Type: application/json
Content-Length: 24
{
  "name": "Gir",
  "animal_type": "12"
}
```

Form URL Encoded

The method shown in Listing 2-17 is used by web sites for accepting simple data forms from a web browser. Data needs to be URL encoded if it contains any special characters (e.g., a space character becomes %20). This is automatically taken care of by the browser.

Listing 2-17. Form URL Encoded Request Body Format

```
POST /login HTTP/1.1
Host: example.com
Content-Length: 31
Accept: text/html
Content-Type: application/x-www-form-urlencoded

username=root&password=Zion0101
```

29

Multipart Form Data

The method shown in Listing 2-18 is used by web sites for accepting more complex data from a web browser such as file uploads. No escaping needs to happen. The boundary is a random string and shouldn't be contained within the uploaded file or form data.

Listing 2-18. Multipart Form Data Request Body Format

```
POST /file_upload HTTP/1.1
Host: example.com
Content-Length: 275
Accept: text/html
Content-Type: multipart/form-data; boundary=-----RANDOM_jDMUxq

------RANDOM_jDMUxq
Content-Disposition: form-data; name="file"; filename="h.txt"
Content-Type: application/octet-stream

Hello World
------RANDOM_jDMUxq
Content-Disposition: form-data; name="some_checkbox"

on
------RANDOM_jDMUxq--
```

HTTP Headers

The first half of the Robustness Principle is to "be liberal in what you accept from others" [8]. According to RFC 2617's Message Headers section, header names are case insensitive [9]. This means you should accept headers from consumers regardless of what the casing is.

A common approach is to iterate over each header, convert it to a consistent case (for example, all lowercase), and then refer to the headers in your application using the same case.

Here are some common headers you can expect your consumers to provide:

- Accept: A list of content types the client accepts

- Accept-Language: The language the client is expecting

- Content-Length: The length of the body in bytes

- Content-Type: The type of data if a body is present

- Host: Used for virtual hosting, usually ignored by application

Headers can be a point of contention for consumers. Whenever possible, try to make them optional or try to allow their options to also be set as query parameters. For example, if your application supports multiple languages and you use the Accept-Language header to select a language, also make use of a &language= parameter. If both are provided, prefer the query parameter because it is typically more intentional (think of someone trying to override their default browser language by changing the URL).

API Responses

There are many ways to convey information to the consumers of your service. By choosing methods that follow well-understood patterns, you can minimize the time it takes developers to get comfortable with your API.

HTTP Status Codes

It is vital that an HTTP API makes use of the proper HTTP status codes; they are a standard after all! Various networking equipment is able to read these status codes (e.g., load balancers can be configured to avoid sending requests to a web server sending out too many errors). Client libraries understand if a request has succeeded or failed depending on the status code.

> The first line of a Response message is the Status-Line, consisting of the protocol version followed by a numeric status code and its associated textual phrase, with each element separated by SP characters. No CR or LF is allowed except in the final CRLF sequence [10].

Listing 2-19 shows an example of what a complete Status-Line header looks like.

Listing 2-19. Example Status-Line

```
HTTP/1.1 404 File Not Found
```

Common API Status Codes

There are a plethora of HTTP status codes to choose from [10], almost to the point of being overwhelming. The following list contains the most common status codes, particularly in the context of API design:

- 200 OK
  - Successful GET/PUT/PATCH requests.
  - The consumer requested data from the server, and the server found it for the consumer.
  - The consumer gave the server data, and the server accepted it.
- 201 Created
  - Successful POST requests.
  - The consumer gave the server data, and the server accepted it.
- 204 No Content
  - Successful DELETE requests.
  - The consumer asked the server to delete a resource, and the server deleted it.

- 400 Invalid Request
  - Erroneous POST/PUT/PATCH requests.
  - The consumer gave bad data to the server, and the server did nothing with it.
- 404 Not Found
  - All requests.
  - The consumer referenced a nonexistent resource or collection.
- 500 Internal Server Error
  - All requests.
  - The server encountered an error, and the consumer does not know whether the request succeeded.

Status Code Ranges

The first digit of the status code is the most significant and provides a generalization of what the entire code is for.

1XX: Informational

The 1XX range is reserved for low-level HTTP happenings, and you'll likely go your entire career without manually sending one of these status codes. An example of this range is when upgrading a connection from HTTP to WebSockets.

2XX: Successful

The 2XX range is reserved for successful responses. Ensure your service sends as many of these to the consumer as possible.

3XX: Redirection

The 3XX range is reserved for traffic redirection, triggering subsequent requests. Most APIs do not use these status codes; however, Hypermedia-style APIs may make more use of them.

4XX: Client Error

The 4XX range is reserved for responding to errors made by the consumer such as when the consumer provides bad data or asks for something that doesn't exist. These requests should be idempotent and not change the state of the server.

5XX: Server Error

The 5XX range is reserved as a response when a service makes a mistake. Oftentimes these errors are created by low-level functions even outside of the developer's control to ensure a consumer gets some sort of response. The consumer can't possibly know the state of the server when a 5XX response is received (e.g., did a failure happen before or after persisting the change?), so these situations should be avoided.

Content Types

Currently the most exciting APIs provide JSON data via HTTP. This includes Facebook, Twitter, GitHub, and so on. Extensible Markup Language (XML) appears to have lost the popularity contest a while ago (save for large corporate environments). SOAP, thankfully, is all but dead. There are not many APIs providing Hypertext Markup Language (HTML) to be consumed.

Figure 2-4 shows a Google Trends graph comparing the terms *JSON API*, *XML API*, and *SOAP API*. This should provide an understanding of how their popularities have changed over time.

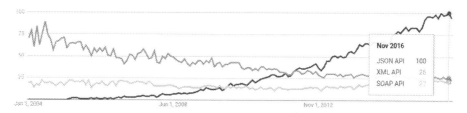

Figure 2-4. *Google Trends graph for JSON API, XML API, and SOAP API*

Developers using popular languages and frameworks can likely parse any valid data format you return to them. You can even interchange data between XML and JSON quite easily if you're building a common response object and swapping serializers. It is crucial that when supporting multiple return formats, you adhere to the Accept header provided by the consumer.

Some API architects recommend adding a .json, .xml, or .html file extension to the URL (appended to the endpoint) for specifying the content type to be returned. Unfortunately, with the different extensions added, you would have different URLs representing the same resources. Use the Accept header, which is built into the HTTP specification specifically for this purpose, and if you can't provide data in a certain format, the consumer requests reply with a 406 Not Acceptable status.

The Accept header has a fallback system where a preferred content type is specified first and lower-priority items follow. Listing 2-20 shows an example of an Accept header provided by the browser.

Listing 2-20. Example Accept Header

```
Accept: text/html, application/xhtml, application/xml;q=0.9
```

In this case, the browser prefers HTML, XHTML, or XML, in that order. There is a standardized syntax for describing fallbacks and how to calculate preferential order outlined in RFC 2616 14.1 [10]. This same syntax is used with the Language header and is worth taking a look at.

Expected Body Content

When a consumer makes a request to the service, something needs to be returned as a response. Depending on the HTTP method and endpoint being requested, the expected responses will differ.

GET /{collection}

When performing a GET request to an entire collection, the consumer typically expects an array of resources to be returned. In the simplest form of HTTP APIs, this consists of a single JSON array containing a homogeneous list of resources, as shown in Listing 2-21.

Listing 2-21. Requesting a Collection

```json
[
  {
    "id": "1",
    "name": "John Smith",
    "created": "2014-01-01T12:00:00Z",
    "modified": null
  },
  {
    "id": "2",
    "name": "Jane Doe",
    "created": "2014-01-01T12:01:00Z",
    "modified": null
  }
]
```

GET /{collection}/{resource_id}

When performing a GET request for a specific resource, the consumer is expecting to receive the resource object. In a simple HTTP API, this is just the resource as a top-level JSON object, such as Listing 2-22.

Listing 2-22. Requesting a Single Resource

```json
{
  "id": "2",
  "name": "Jane Doe",
  "created": "2014-01-01T12:01:00Z",
  "modified": null
}
```

POST /{collection}

When performing a POST request to a collection, the consumer expects the resource it just created to be returned. In an ideal RESTful API, the resource being provided is the same as the resource being returned. However, there is important information being returned to the consumer that it doesn't already know such as a resource identifier and other calculated attributes such as timestamps. Listing 2-23 shows an example response you can provide.

Listing 2-23. Creating a Resource

```
{
  "id": "3",
  "name": "Alice Roberts",
  "created": "2014-01-01T12:02:00Z",
  "modified": null
}
```

PUT /{collection}/{resource_id}

The result of a PUT operation is the entirety of the resource that was updated as the root JSON object. Listing 2-24 shows an example.

Listing 2-24. Updating a Resource

```
{
  "id": "3",
  "name": "Alice Smith",
  "created": "2014-01-01T12:01:00Z",
  "modified": "2014-01-01T12:03:00Z"
}
```

PATCH /{collection}/{resource_id}

The result of a PATCH request is the same as the result of a PUT operation. Even though the consumer may have acted on only some of the attributes, the entire resource should be returned. For completeness, this is shown in Listing 2-25.

Listing 2-25. Partially Updating a Resource

```
{
  "id": "3",
  "name": "Alicia Smith",
  "created": "2014-01-01T12:01:00Z",
  "modified": "2014-01-01T12:04:00Z"
}
```

DELETE /{collection}/{resource_id}

This is the easiest of the bodies to deal with. Once a resource is deleted, you simply return an empty document. There's no need to return information about the deleted resource. Since no body is present, you can omit the `Content-Type` header.

It may be convenient for the consumer if you reply with a representation of the deleted resource in the body of the response. This would allow the consumer to display information about the deleted resource without needing to precede the DELETE request with a GET. In this situation, you would want to provide the `Content-Type` header.

JSON Attribute Conventions

JSON is a subset of JavaScript and was defined for the purpose of building a language-agnostic data interchange format. It fills mostly the same role that XML was designed to fill except that it has the side effect of being much more compact and easily deserializes into native objects in most languages. It also supports many different data types, whereas XML technically only supports strings without the inclusion of metadata.

That said, there is still quite a bit of freedom that a developer has when representing data using JSON. This section of the book is designed to give you advice for representing data.

Attribute Name Casing

When providing JSON data, a service needs to be consistent about the case it uses. There are a few common approaches; pick the one that works best for your team and run with it. No format is better or worse than the other; it's really all based on preferences. Of course, you should use the same format for the request bodies that you accept from consumers.

> **Collaboration Tip**: Regardless of the style you choose, try to adopt a single style across your organization.

Snake Case

Snake case, shown in Listing 2-26, uses lowercase words with underscores to separate them. This format uses the most bytes and seems to be the most common approach used in RESTful JSON APIs. For example, GitHub and Stripe follow this approach.

Listing 2-26. Snake Case

```
{
  "id": "alice",
  "first_name": "Alice"
}
```

Pascal Case

Pascal case, shown in Listing 2-27, uses a capital letter for all words. This format seems to be most common in the Microsoft .NET/enterprise world.

Listing 2-27. Pascal Case

```
{
  "Id": "alice",
  "FirstName": "Alice"
}
```

Camel Case

Camel case, shown in Listing 2-28, uses a capital letter for all words except for the first one. This minimizes the number of times a developer has to press Shift.

Listing 2-28. Camel Case

```
{
  "id": "alice",
  "firstName": "Alice"
}
```

Consistency Between Resources

Whenever you represent different resources within the same collection, each attribute should remain the same data type. For example, if one resource has an id attribute that is a string, you shouldn't in a different resource represent it as an integer.

There are some exceptions to this; for example, when a value doesn't exist, it should be represented as a null. In general, keeping the attributes of the same data type will make your API easier for consumers to use, especially those using statically typed languages. (JavaScript and PHP are more forgiving in this regard. Languages such as C# or Java will likely create a class for every type of object encountered.)

Booleans

It may be tempting to name your Booleans with a prefix or suffix to symbolize the purpose of the attribute. Common examples of this would be to prefix the variable with is_ or end it with _flag.

This really isn't necessary because attribute names are often self-documenting. For example, if there is an attribute on your User resource called administrator, it should be obvious that using a non-Boolean isn't intended.

Another tip with Booleans is that they should usually be positive or happy words as opposed to their negative counterparts. This will prevent developers from having to figure out a double negative. For example, use enabled instead of disabled, public instead of private, and even keep instead of purge.

Timestamps

There are a multitude of standards for representing dates and times.

ISO 8601

The ideal standard for representing dates is the ISO 8601 standard [11], and it looks a bit like Listing 2-29.

Listing 2-29. ISO 8601

```
"2014-01-10T03:06:17.396Z"
"2014-01-09T22:06:17+05:00"
```

This format is human-readable, lacks redundant information, has variable precision (the microseconds on the end is optional), conveys time zone information (the Z in the first example means UTC, but an offset can be provided, as shown in the second example), and is the most popular of standardized date formats. Assuming several values each use the same time zone, then their alphabetical ordering is also chronological.

JavaScript Default

JSON is a subset of JavaScript, and JavaScript does have a default format for parsing dates. To see this format generated, create a new Date object and convert it to a String object. The format of these dates looks like Listing 2-30.

Listing 2-30. JavaScript Default

```
"Thu Jan 09 2014 22:06:17 GMT-0500 (EST)"
```

Unfortunately, this format is a verbose eyesore. Who cares what day of the week it was? Avoid this format at all costs.

Unix Epoch

If you wanted something much terser, you could represent the date as the number of seconds (or milliseconds) since January 1, 1970. This value can be transmitted as an integer, as shown in Listing 2-31.

Listing 2-31. Unix Epoch

```
1493268311
1493268311123
```

This format is a bit too terse. As a human looking at it, you have no idea what date and time it represents! Linux and Unix machines and open source languages can parse that format easily; however, developers using Microsoft technology may be left scratching their heads.

The number is always assumed to be in UTC time, so there's no issue in that regard. There is, however, some ambiguity as to whether milliseconds have been included; the true Unix epoch time value is in seconds, but many prefer to use the more accurate representation.

SQL Timestamp

Listing 2-32 contains an example of another common date format. This is what happens when a developer takes a timestamp directly from a SQL database and outputs it into the response.

Listing 2-32. SQL Timestamp

```
"2014-01-10 03:06:17"
```

The problem with this format is that it does not convey what time zone the date is in! You may be tempted to use this format and document the time zone of the server (which is referred to as being *out of band*). However, developers will not remember it, and users of their application will wonder why a newly uploaded image has a modified time of five hours and three seconds ago.

Resource Identifiers (IDs)

Whenever communicating IDs, transfer them as strings (even if they are numeric). Everything a consumer does with an ID is in string form anyway. If they make a request to the resource, the ID is concatenated with another string and used as a URL. If the ID is logged, it is written as a string on disk. And unless the consumer is doing some questionable scraping of your API, the ID should never need to have arithmetic performed with it.

Also, if IDs are always sent as a string, deciding to change from a numeric representation to a different format such as a UUID (e.g., 7d531700-79a5-11e3-979a-a79bcbe406e9) or a Base62-encoded value (e.g., oHg5SJYRHA0) will result in no code changes on the consumer's end.

There are two common families when it comes to keeping track of IDs. The first family is incremental (such as an integer), while the second is random (such as a UUID). There are different use cases for the two types of IDs. Random IDs are useful when you don't want a third party to know how many resources you have, when you don't want a third party to easily guess ID values (e.g., scrape your data), or when IDs are being generated by many systems in parallel and you don't want the overhead of checking uniqueness. Incremental IDs are useful when you create resources in a central location or when you want the smallest-sized IDs (e.g., in bytes) possible.

Nulls

If most resources have a particular attribute available and some do not, you should always provide the attribute in the document with a null value instead of outright omitting it.

This will make things easier for consumers who won't need to check whether a JSON attribute exists before attempting to read it.

Arrays

When representing resources with attributes that represent an array, you should give the attribute a plural name. This signifies to the developer they should expect more than one value.

When an array shouldn't have any entries, you should typically return an array with nothing in it, instead of returning a null.

Whitespace

Whitespace, while convenient for a human to read, isn't beneficial to a consumer and incurs some extra networking overhead. JSON visualization tools will add whitespace and perform syntax highlighting anyway. It's really up to you to decide whether you want to add whitespace to the output.

JSON allows for any amount of whitespace between keys and values, but if you are going to add whitespace, use a simple and consistent standard. Two spaces for indentation and a single newline is common practice.

Error Reporting

Errors are an inevitability of any cross-service communication. Users will fat finger an e-mail address, developers will not read the tiny disclaimer you hid in your API documentation, and a database server will occasionally burst into flames. When this happens, the server will of course return a 4XX or 5XX HTTP status code, but the document body itself should have useful information included.

When designing an error object, there isn't a specific standard that you need to follow. The examples that follow aren't an existing standard, but feel free to use them as a starting point when designing your own errors. Make sure that there is consistency between errors regardless of the endpoint.

There are essentially two classes of errors you can account for. The first one is a simple error where it is easy to point to a specific attribute as being the problem. Let's refer to these as validation errors. The second class of errors is a bit more complex and may not be easily interpreted by an API consumer. Let's call these generic errors.

Validation Errors

When an error happens regarding a malformed attribute, such as in Listing 2-33, provide the consumer with a reference to the attribute causing the error as well as a message about what is wrong, as in Listing 2-34. Assuming the consumer is providing a user interface (UI) for a user to input data, the UI can display the message for the user to read as well as provide context for the user.

Listing 2-33. Erroneous Request

```
PUT /v1/users/1

{
  "name": "Rupert Styx",
  "age": "Twenty Eight"
}
```

Listing 2-34. Validation Error Response

```
HTTP/1.1 400 Bad Request

{
  "error_human": "Inputs not formatted as expected",
  "error_code": "invalid_attributes",
  "fields": [
    {
      "field": "age",
      "error_human":"Age must be a number between 1 and 100",
      "error_code": "integer_validation"
    }
  ]
}
```

Generic Errors

When an error occurs that can't be traced back to a single input attribute being incorrect, you'll want to return a more generic error construct. In Listing 2-35 you see an otherwise fine request, but for unforeseen reasons you get the server error in Listing 2-36.

Listing 2-35. Request

```
POST /v1/animals

{
  "name": "Mittens",
  "type": "kitten"
}
```

Listing 2-36. Generic Error Response

```
HTTP/1.1 503 Service Unavailable

{
  "error_human": "The Database is currently unavailable.",
  "error_code": "database_unavailable"
}
```

Always Handle Server Errors

Make sure you catch all errors your server is capable of producing and *always* return content to the consumer in the format the consumer is expecting!

This sounds obvious, but it can actually be a lot harder than you think. In PHP, for example, extra care has to be made to catch all errors. By default PHP and many other web languages/frameworks will return HTML-formatted errors.

Consumers will throw all sorts of broken data your way. Experiment with your server and see what sort of errors you can cause it to produce. Try sending malformed JSON, upload a 100GB file, corrupt the HTTP headers, make 100,000 concurrent requests, and even try removing the underlying code or breaking file permissions and see how your web server handles it.

String-Based Error Codes

In my opinion there are two types of strings in programming. The first type of string contains human-readable text that includes punctuation and different letter cases and even Unicode symbols. These strings should never be used for comparison. When I program in a language that supports both single and double quotes for strings, I'll surround these in double quotes as a reminder.

The other types of strings are computer-readable strings. These are much simpler, are often used for attributes (you wouldn't use `First Name` as a JSON key, would you?), and should be all lowercase and contain underscores (or camel case, if you're one of *those* people). These strings could pass as names of variables in most languages. I'll usually surround these strings in single quotes.

Returning to the topic of error codes, it is important to provide the consumer with *both* a computer-readable error code as well as a human-readable error message. The code can be compared in a conditional and have logic applied to it by the consumer. The human-readable message can change at any point if a translation changes or any type of rewrite happens without breaking logic.

Many APIs I've seen include the use of numeric error codes. For example, if there was an error with a database transaction being committed, the error code might be 2091. A third-party developer working with the API and coming across that error is going to have absolutely no idea what that number means and will have to go look it up in the API docs (the meaning is out of band). If that message were instead `database_transaction_failure`, the developer is going to have somewhat of a clue as to what just happened and will be able to compensate faster.

The Stripe API [12] makes great use of error strings for conveying error codes. One such example is `expired_card`, which as a third-party developer you immediately know that the user-supplied card has expired.

Responses Should Mimic Requests

As a general rule, a response resource structure should closely resemble the equivalent request resource. This means the same attribute names and values are used for requests as well as responses.

There are, of course, a few exceptions. A PATCH, for example, affects only a partial document. A POST won't have certain server-calculated attributes (such as an ID or a created timestamp). PATCHes and PUTs won't have certain read-only attributes (e.g., created and modified times). These differences in attributes should be minimal when possible.

Whenever dealing with the values of attributes, they should always be the same format. A good philosophy to follow is that request objects should be a strict subset of response objects.

Acceptable Discrepancy

In this example, the differences between the request (Listing 2-37) and the response (Listing 2-38) documents are minimal. Some of the values are read-only and calculated on the server (e.g., id, modified, and created). Some of the attributes have default values (e.g., enabled), which is fine as long as these are documented.

Listing 2-37. Request

```
POST /users

{
  "role": "administrator",
  "name": "Rupert Styx"
}
```

Listing 2-38. Response with Acceptable Discrepancy

```
{
  "id": "12",
  "role": "administrator",
  "created": "2014-01-15T02:40:46.049Z",
  "modified": null,
  "name": "Rupert Styx",
  "enabled": true
}
```

Avoidable Discrepancy

In this example, during a POST to the users endpoint (Listing 2-39), there is a role attribute that is a string containing possible user roles such as administrator or moderator. However, in the response (Listing 2-40), that same data becomes a Boolean of whether the user is an administrator. This increases the amount of attribute names the consumer needs to keep track of.

43

Listing 2-39. Request

```
POST /users

{
  "role": "administrator",
  "name": "Rupert Styx"
}
```

Listing 2-40. Response with Avoidable Discrepancy

```
{
  "id": "12",
  "administrator": true,
  "name": "Rupert Styx"
}
```

HTTP Headers

The second half of the Robustness principle [8] is "be conservative in what you do." While it is true that HTTP allows headers to be of any case, it is best to be diligent and provide a consistent casing for your headers. Throughout the HTTP specification you'll find examples using Uppercase-And-Hyphens, and I recommend your application responds using the same.

Headers are useful for providing meta-information to consumers about their requests. The following are common headers that you should almost always provide in your responses:

- Cache-Control: Used for setting cache policy (e.g., no-cache)

- Content-Length: Number of bytes in body

- Content-Type: Type of content such as application/json

- Date: The date and time on the server

- Expires: Time when content should expire

- Server: A useless field servers use for bragging

API Standards

So far, all the example response bodies have been simple representations of resources or arrays of resources. There is important meta-information that you could be providing as well as intrinsic methods for describing the purpose of data.

Simple Response Envelope

When responding with a document representing, say, a collection, it is usually adequate to return a top-level array containing each resource object. Likewise, when responding with a document representing a resource, simply returning a top-level object containing the resource is usually good enough.

However, there are some standards that forward-thinking API architects have developed for encapsulating these objects in a standardized envelope. These envelopes give the consumer context when parsing the responses.

For example, if making a filtered request limits a collection response to contain only ten resources, how do you let the consumer know how many total records exist? How do you convey expected data types programmatically? If a consumer is expecting an array of resources and you provide an error object, how will the consumer handle it? These different response document standards provide methods for returning this metadata.

Listing 2-41 shows an example of one such envelope you could use in your application.

Listing 2-41. Simple Envelope with a Single Resource

```
{
  "type": "single",
  "error": null,
  "error_human": null,
  "data": {
    "id": 1
  }
}
```

Listing 2-42 applies the same envelope format for a collection of resources.

Listing 2-42. Simple Envelope with a Collection of Resources

```
{
  "type": "collection",
  "error": null,
  "error_human": null,
  "data": [
    {
      "id": "10"
    },
    {
      "id": "11"
    }
  ],
  "offset": 10,
  "per_page": 10
}
```

Listing 2-43 shows how this same envelope could be used to convey an error.

Listing 2-43. Simple Envelope with Error

```
{
  "error": "database_connection_failed",
  "error_human": "Unable to establish database connection",
  "data": null
}
```

JSON Schema

JSON Schema [13] provides a method for describing the attributes provided by an API endpoint. This description is written in JSON in such a way as to be both human-readable and easy to work with programmatically. Using JSON Schema, a consumer could easily automate data validation and generation of CRUD forms. Listing 2-44 shows an example of a JSON Schema document.

Listing 2-44. Example JSON Schema Document

```
{
  "title": "Example Schema",
  "type": "object",
  "properties": {
    "firstName": {
      "type": "string"
    },
    "lastName": {
      "type": "string"
    },
    "age": {
      "description": "Age in years",
      "type": "integer",
      "minimum": 0
    }
  },
  "required": ["firstName", "lastName"]
}
```

JSON API

The JSON API [14] spec provided a standardized format for structuring response documents by introducing some reserved attributes that have special meaning (e.g., id must be used for identifying a resource, a convention you've already been following throughout this book).

A notable feature of JSON API is that it also provides a method for returning not only a requested resource but also other resources that it depends on as if anticipating the consumer's next request (or requests). Listing 2-45 provides an example JSON API document.

Listing 2-45. Example JSON API Document

```json
{
  "links": {
    "posts.author": {
      "href": "http://example.com/people/{posts.author}",
      "type": "people"
    },
    "posts.comments": {
      "href": "http://example.com/comments/{posts.comments}",
      "type": "comments"
    }
  },
  "posts": [{
    "id": "1",
    "title": "Rails is Omakase",
    "links": {
      "author": "9",
      "comments": [ "1", "2" ]
    }
  }],
  "linked": {
    "people": [{
      "id": "9",
      "name": "@d2h"
    }],
    "comments": [{
      "id": "1",
      "body": "Mmmmmakase"
    }, {
      "id": "2",
      "body": "I prefer unagi"
    }]
  }
}
```

GraphQL

GraphQL [15] is an API specification created by Facebook. It requires the use of a unique query language as well as a similar language for defining schemas. The data returned is typically formatted as JSON though it doesn't enforce a format. GraphQL makes use of a single HTTP endpoint.

What really makes GraphQL unique is the way it allows you to define relationships between resources and then receive multiple resources using a single query, a feature that a purely RESTful approach can't account for.

As an example of this, imagine you want to get information about a particular user as well as all of the friends of the user. You would also like to get the profile photo of the user. In a RESTful API, you may need to make the three different queries shown in Listing 2-46.

Listing 2-46. Multiple Requests Without GraphQL

```
GET {user_api}/users/tlhunter?whitelist=id,name,photo_id
GET {user_api}/users/tlhunter/friends?whitelist=id,name
GET {photo_api}/photos/12345/profile
```

This process can be painful because you need to make several queries and white-list the data you want to receive. Some of these requests can be made in parallel; however, for the profile photo, you first need to get the photo_id from the user's endpoint. If these requests were being made from a mobile device to your APIs, there would be many chances for failure.

Here's how you can solve this issue using GraphQL. First you need models for representing the different types of resources, in this case a user and a photo, as shown in Listing 2-47.

Listing 2-47. GraphQL Model Syntax

```
type User {
  id: ID!
  photo_id: String!
  name: String
  friends: [User]
}
type Photo {
  id: ID!
  url: String
}
```

You can then query this data using the GraphQL query shown in Listing 2-48.

Listing 2-48. GraphQL Query Syntax

```
{
  user(id: "tlhunter") {
    id
    name
    photo {
      id
      url
    }
    friends {
      id
      name
    }
  }
}
```

Finally, the data is provided to you in a familiar JSON format, as shown in Listing 2-49.

Listing 2-49. GraphQL JSON Result

```
{
  "data": {
    "user": {
      "name": "Thomas Hunter II",
      "id": "tlhunter",
      "photo": {
        "id": 12345,
        "url": "http://im.example.org/12345.jpg"
      },
      "friends": [
        {
          "name": "Rupert Styx",
          "id": "rupertstyx"
        }
      ]
    }
  }
}
```

GraphQL is useful for both APIs exposed within the company and ones that are publically accessible. It is particularly well-suited for the task of building an API facade, which is an API that abstracts other APIs and provides a single place to get the data you need.

GraphQL provides many more features than what I've covered in this section such as the ability to write changes. The model syntax is also much richer. For more information, check out the GraphpQL documentation [15].

Hypermedia APIs

It would be irresponsible to cover HTTP-based API design without mentioning Hypermedia/Representational State Transfer (REST) [16]. Hypermedia APIs may very well be the future of HTTP API design. It really is an amazing concept going back to the roots of how HTTP (and HTML) was intended to work.

With the examples I've been covering up to this point, the URL endpoints are part of the contract between the API and the consumer. These endpoints must be known by the consumer ahead of time, and changing them means the consumer is no longer able to communicate with the API.

API consumers are far from being the only user agent making HTTP requests on the Internet. Humans with their web browsers are the most common user agent making HTTP requests. Humans, of course, are *not* locked into this predefined endpoint URL contract that most HTTP APIs are.

What makes humans so special? We're able to read content, click links for headings that look interesting, and in general explore a web site and interpret content to get where we want to go. If a URL changes, we're not affected (unless we bookmarked a page, in which case we go to the home page and find a new route to our beloved article).

The Hypermedia API concept works the same way a human would. Requesting the root of the API returns a listing of URLs that point perhaps to each collection of information, describing each collection in a way that the consumer can understand. Providing IDs for each resource isn't important as long as a URL to the resource is provided.

With the consumer of a Hypermedia API crawling links and gathering information, URLs are always up-to-date within responses and do not need to be known as part of a contract. If a URL is ever cached and a subsequent request returns a 404 error, the consumer can simply go back to the root and discover the content again.

When retrieving a list of resources within a collection, an attribute containing a complete URL for the individual resources is returned. When performing a POST/PATCH/PUT, the response could be a 3XX redirect to the complete resource.

JSON doesn't quite give you the semantics you need for specifying which attributes are URLs or how URLs relate to the current document (although, as you'll soon see, there are some standards for doing this). HTML, as you should already know, does provide this information! You may very well see your APIs come full circle and return to consuming HTML. Considering how far we've come with Cascading Style Sheets (CSS), one day it may be common practice for APIs and web sites to use the same URLs and HTML content.

Imagine a tool on the Internet that you want to use. It could be Google Calendar, Meetup, or Facebook Events. Also imagine that you want to use other tools too, such as e-mail or instant messengers. Normally integrations between tools are convenient only if you're using a massive suite of tools such as what is offered by Microsoft or Google. As an example, Google Mail integrates very tightly with Google Calendar and Google+ to provide a seamless user experience.

Now imagine that the disparate tools by different companies can work with each other as tightly as these massive suites of tools. Oftentimes when a company builds a single product, it is better than the equivalent component of a larger suite. This combination of specific, well-built tools working seamlessly with other services becomes the best of both worlds! The process could theoretically work automatically with the different services discovering each other and configuring themselves to play nicely. This is a feature offered by Hypermedia-based APIs.

ATOM [17], a distant cousin of RSS, is likely one of the first mainstream Hypermedia APIs (other than HTML itself). ATOM is valid XML and therefore relatively easy to parse. Links to other documents use a link tag and specify both the URL (using the `href` attribute) and the document's relation to the current document (using the `rel` attribute). You can see an example ATOM document in Listing 2-50.

Listing 2-50. Example ATOM Document

```
<?xml version="1.0" encoding="utf-8"?>
<feed xmlns="http://www.w3.org/2005/Atom">
  <title>Example Feed</title>
  <subtitle>A subtitle.</subtitle>
  <link href="http://example.org/feed/" rel="self" />
  <link href="http://example.org/" />
  <id>urn:uuid:60a76c80-d399-11d9-b91C-0003939e0af6</id>
  <updated>2003-12-13T18:30:02Z</updated>
  <entry>
    <title>Atom-Powered Robots Run Amok</title>
    <link href="http://example.org/2003/12/13/atom03" />
    <link rel="alternate" type="text/html"
        href="http://example.org/2003/12/13/atom03.html"/>
    <link rel="edit"
        href="http://example.org/2003/12/13/atom03/edit"/>
    <id>urn:uuid:1225c695-cfb8-4ebb-aaaa-80da344efa6a</id>
    <updated>2003-12-13T18:30:02Z</updated>
    <summary>Some text.</summary>
    <author>
      <name>John Doe</name>
      <email>johndoe@example.com</email>
    </author>
  </entry>
</feed>
```

API Transports

Up until now I've placed a large emphasis on the importance of a URL in your HTTP-based APIs. However, there are some standards you should be aware of that have a small emphasis on the URL, typically serving all requests through a single URL.

You will also explore situations where you need not use HTTP at all to communicate. Using a different protocol such as Transmission Control Protocol (TCP) or User Datagram Protocol (UDP), you can get rid of some of the overhead of HTTP. You can even transport data using binary formats, which will result in less data sent over the network.

JSON RPC

JSON RPC [18] is a relatively popular alternative to REST for exposing functionality over a network. Whereas REST is required to be accessed via HTTP, JSON RPC doesn't have a protocol requirement. It can be sent over sockets, can be used with Inter Process Communication (IPC), and of course can be used with HTTP.

Unlike REST, which requires an abstraction of server business logic and data into simple resource objects that can be acted upon using CRUD, JSON RPC calls will typically map to existing functions within your application.

51

When a client makes a call using JSON RPC, the client specifies the name of a function to execute as well as arguments to the function. Arguments can be in the form of either ordered parameters (using a JSON array) or named parameters (using a JSON object).

The important part of the specification is the envelope that the data adheres to. The concept of a URL doesn't really exist (if you're using JSON RPC over HTTP, there's usually a single URL that all requests are sent through, and each request is likely sent as a POST).

JSON RPC is mostly useful for situations where you don't have an HTTP server such as multiplayer games or embedded systems or simple communication applications. If you already have an HTTP server for your product or service, REST is likely a better solution for you.

With HTTP, every request and response is guaranteed to be paired correctly. Because of the asynchronous nature of sockets and other such communication protocols, requests need to provide a unique ID value, and the corresponding response needs to provide the same ID.

JSON RPC also has mechanisms for sending batches of operations at once and in some situations can complement a RESTful API.

Listing 2-51 shows an example of a JSON RPC request, and Listing 2-52 shows its correlating response.

Listing 2-51. Example JSON RPC Request

```
{"jsonrpc":"2.0","method":"subtract","params":[42,23],"id":1}
```

Listing 2-52. Example JSON RPC Response

```
{"jsonrpc": "2.0", "result": 19, "id": 1}
```

SOAP

Worth mentioning is Simple Object Access Protocol (SOAP), which is a term you may have heard of [19]. SOAP is a sort of successor to an older technology called XML RPC. As you've probably guessed, XML RPC is similar to JSON RPC because both are forms of Remote Procedure Call protocols.

SOAP is useful for describing services exposed over the network and is transport agnostic just like JSON RPC, although most implementations use it over HTTP. Partly because of the waning popularity of XML in comparison to JSON, SOAP is often looked down upon due to the verbosity and the bulkiness of document sizes.

SOAP is mostly used in larger, corporate environments. Listing 2-53 shows an example of a SOAP request.

Listing 2-53. Example SOAP Request

```
<?xml version="1.0"?>
<soap:Envelope
    xmlns:soap="http://www.w3.org/2003/05/soap-envelope">
  <soap:Header>
  </soap:Header>
```

```
 <soap:Body>
  <m:GetStockPrice xmlns:m="http://www.example.org/stock">
     <m:StockName>IBM</m:StockName>
  </m:GetStockPrice>
 </soap:Body>
</soap:Envelope>
```

MessagePack (Binary)

So far you've been learning about only text-based formats for sending data over the wire with an emphasis on JSON and a look at XML. Text is great because it can be read by a human and follows the Unix philosophy [20] of text being the universal interface.

There are also costs involved with serialization and deserialization of data to text because you need to take complex objects in memory and convert them into a large concatenated string. This can be processing and memory intensive for a producer and even become a bottleneck. This is where binary formats come to the rescue.

MessagePack is *schemaless* (much like JSON itself), and serialization from JSON-like objects (Listing 2-54) to a MessagePack representation (Listing 2-55) is straightforward. There are markers/flags that explain how the data that follows is structured.

Listing 2-54. JSON Representation

```
{"id": "tlhunter", "xyz": [1,2,3]}
```

Listing 2-55. MessagePack Serialization

```
82 a2 69 64 a8 74 6c 68 75 6e 74
65 72 a3 78 79 7a 93 01 02 03
```

In this representation each pair of hexadecimal numbers represents a single byte. I'm printing them in this manner because it's the only way to represent binary data in a book.

The first byte in Listing 2-55, 82, means the data is a two-element map (the id and xyz properties). Add a third item, and the entry becomes 83.

The a2 means the next item is a two-byte string, id. And of course if it were three bytes, it would be a3.

Notice how the last three bytes in the MessagePack representation are 01, 02, 03 and how the last three items in JSON are the numbers 1, 2, 3. Coincidence? I think not.

However, with MessagePack being schemaless, it misses out on valuable information about your data. A common situation is where you repeat similar objects, with the JSON object in Listing 2-56 being serialized into Listing 2-57.

Listing 2-56. JSON Representation

```
[
  {"message": false},
  {"message": true},
  {"message": false}
]
```

Listing 2-57. MessagePack Serialization

```
93
81 a7 6d 65 73 73 61 67 65
c2
81 a7 6d 65 73 73 61 67 65
c3
81 a7 6d 65 73 73 61 67 65
c2
```

In the resulting object in Listing 2-57 (ignore the newlines, which add clarity), notice how the bytes 6d 65 73 73 61 67 65 (message) are repeated three times. While the overall message contains fewer bytes than the JSON version, it's still not as efficient as it could be.

For more information about how data is represented or to find a library for your language of choice, check out the MessagePack web site [21].

Apache Thrift (Binary)

Unlike MessagePack, Thrift does follow a schema. This means data has to be described as an object (enum) ahead of time. This description of how the data is structured then needs to be shared among all nodes that will consume or produce the data. Thrift has tools for generating these schemas and libraries for loading them in your application.

The benefits of Thrift are that the amount of data sent on the network will be smaller than with MessagePack. Attribute names don't need to be sent in a payload because they need to exist only in the schema. Think of this like a CSV file where the first line contains the names of columns and no subsequent lines need the column names. It is also much more difficult to violate contracts between provider and consumer because of these schemas.

Of course, this comes with a loss of flexibility. Schemas are generated ahead of time, need to be versioned, and need to be available to both the provider and the consumer.

CHAPTER 3

Deployments

Deploying an application to a production environment with confidence that it isn't going to crash or otherwise lose your organization money is something all developers should strive for. Automating as much of this as you can will help reduce human error.

In this chapter, you'll look at testing your service, wrapping it up as a container, running tests, and deploying to different environments using container orchestration tools.

Automated Testing

Before talking about deploying your code, I need to first talk about testing your code. Deploying code that you are not confident will work is dangerous. You need to be able to run a variety of tests against your code, everything from the lowly unit test that covers individual functions to acceptance tests that ensure a whole system is functioning.

Tests should be as easy to run as executing a command within the working directory of your project. This will make it easy both for humans and for automated testing software to run tests.

Unit Tests

Unit tests are the most basic level of testing you can use in a project. These tests run individual functions within your codebase, passing in different parameters to ensure each branch of code in the function runs.

This is also the level where developers are usually checking code coverage. All popular modern languages have tools for testing code coverage as unit tests run. As a rule of thumb, the closer you approach 100 percent code coverage, the closer you approach 100 percent confidence in your code.

In your project, set up a threshold for code coverage. New pull requests that add features but do not test features will lower the overall coverage level and cause a failure. This makes for an excellent reason to deny a contribution.

© Thomas Hunter II 2017
T. Hunter II, *Advanced Microservices*, DOI 10.1007/978-1-4842-2887-6_3

Smoke Tests

Smoke tests are used as a sanity check in the testing process before running other types of tests. In particular, they are useful for talking to services outside of your own to ensure those services are functioning as expected.

If the smoke tests fail, you know that you shouldn't bother running your tests that talk to other services. If you don't use smoke tests, then you can assume that failed tests are because of faulty code when it may in fact be because of someone else's project.

Integration Tests

Integration tests are useful for checking how larger parts of the system work together. While a unit test may ensure that the input and output of a single function is correct, an integration test will ensure that the output of a function is compatible with the input of another function.

You may even check that your service functions properly with other services. This could include making connections to databases, caching services, or making outbound requests to other services within the organization. These types of tests usually end up being the "flakiest" because real-world network and data issues can affect the outcome of the tests.

Acceptance Tests

Acceptance tests check that the particular needs of the business are being fulfilled by the application. An individual acceptance test can be as complex as a user story or as simple as a single interaction. For example, if a service has a parameter that sorts results, then a relevant acceptance test would be to make a request with the parameter and ensure results are sorted properly.

If a service has a web interface, it's not uncommon to create a headless browser instance, make a request to a web page, click elements, and ensure that the expected data comes back. This may require the service to communicate with other services, such as an integration test, or instead make use of mock data.

Performance Tests

It's a good idea to keep track of performance data with each test run. Perhaps you have a certain set of requests that are frequently made in groups such as the flow of a user signing up and authenticating and making a purchase. By benchmarking these requests and then running them hundreds of times in a row, you can see whether new commits are slowing you down. Set a threshold and fail a contribution if it makes the service too slow.

Regression Tests

Regression testing is used to ensure that code that used to work will still work after changes have been made. This could mean running all the other tests every single time you make changes. It could also mean running any subset of those tests. Many large organizations will find themselves with teams of quality assurance (QA) experts who may even write their own tests and run them against your software over and over.

Containers

Before talking about containers, let's take a quick look at a situation without them.

In Figure 3-1 you can see how applications have typically been run on servers. Each layer in this diagram represents an added layer of overhead such as random access memory (RAM) usage. In this example, an operating system runs directly on hardware. Various libraries (and other dependencies) required by applications are installed on the operating system (OS). You run your applications directly on this OS. If a library is used by multiple applications, then the libraries are shared; each library only needs to exist on disk (and possibly in memory) once. The overall resource overhead with this approach is minimal.

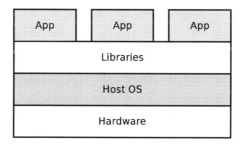

No Virtualization

Figure 3-1. No containers or virtual machines

This approach has drawbacks, however. Installing system libraries can be a hassle, especially when you want deterministic installs. Applications are usually going to require that libraries of an exact version are installed, and different applications may require different versions of libraries. Consider the situation where Application A requires Python 2 and Application B requires Python 3.

Satisfying the dependency requirements of multiple apps simultaneously is difficult. Dynamically spawning applications on operating systems without the necessary dependency installed is also difficult; you would need to install the dependencies before every deployment (and library installations can be a slow process). Luckily, you can use containers to simplify this process.

Containers are a convenient method for taking an application and completely isolating it from other applications within a single operating system. Applications isolated in this manner are only able to interact outside of their containers in highly configurable ways. Containers will typically have access to their own filesystems and their own process ID (PID) space and can listen on whatever port they want without having to worry about conflicting with other containers.

Applications shipped inside a container will need to come bundled with every library and configuration script that the application depends on. Applications are able to communicate with the kernel using system calls. This allows you to decouple an application from the Linux distribution it depends on, allowing you to run the application the same regardless of the library versions and configuration of the host OS.

Virtual machines are another way to achieve even more extreme isolation; however, these come with the overhead of running a redundant kernel for every virtual machine (VM). Figure 3-2 shows this duplication of OSs when using only virtual machines. For this reason, containers are better for running individual applications, whereas VMs are better for running (multiple) containers.

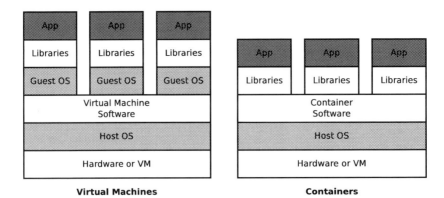

Figure 3-2. *Containers versus virtual machines*

Docker Containers

Docker [22] is currently the most popular container solution. It offers a lot of features and is supported by many third-party systems such as orchestration tools. Docker depends on a Linux kernel; in other words, to run it on Windows or macOS, you need to run it inside some sort of virtual machine containing the Linux kernel. If, like me, you've eschewed these popular consumer operating systems, you're then free to run it directly on your development machine.

Configuring Docker images requires the creation of a configuration file, which will sit at the root of your project and is called the Dockerfile. This is a text file that describes the requirements of your project such as a base image to run on (e.g., one that provides Node. js binaries), commands to run (e.g., installation), a port the app will listen on, and so on.

Docker images have a sort of dependency system to them. An image can extend another image, which itself can extend another one. When performing installations, Docker will download each layer and cache them so that subsequent installs will be quicker. These images are then stacked on each other thanks to UnionFS [23]. This allows each image's filesystems to be merged, forming a cohesive, ideally completely functioning system.

While it's true that Docker uses the kernel of the host, you will frequently see images depend on a Linux distribution, as in debian:jessie. Since Linux is really just the Linux kernel and different distributions use this same kernel (though modifications can happen), these images simply contain "userland" files. As an example, Debian will provide a filesystem with /srv, /var, common binaries, and so on.

Dockerfile Breakdown

Let's take a look at the Dockerfile used by MongoDB. This file, provided in Listing 3-1, comes from the official Dockerfile GitHub account. This account contains files for many popular open source projects.

Listing 3-1. Dockerfile from MongoDB

```
FROM dockerfile/ubuntu

RUN \
  apt-key adv --keyserver hkp://keyserver.ubuntu.com:80 \
  --recv 7F0CEB10 && \
  echo "deb http://downloads-distro.mongodb.org/repo/\
ubuntu-upstart dist 10gen" > \
  /etc/apt/sources.list.d/mongodb.list && \
  apt-get update && \
  apt-get install -y mongodb-org && \
  rm -rf /var/lib/apt/lists/*

VOLUME ["/data/db"]

WORKDIR /data

CMD ["mongod"]

EXPOSE 27017
EXPOSE 28017
```

The FROM directive tells Docker what the base image is. This image (and its dependencies) will be used to generate the final MongoDB image.

The RUN directive tells Docker to execute these commands (as root) inside of the image. The commands used in this case are instructing Ubuntu to accept an encryption key used for signing the MongoDB packages by its company, 10gen, as well as instructing the package manager to add the MongoDB package repository. It then has Ubuntu update its list of packages and installs MongoDB.

The VOLUME directive has Docker mount a directory within the image that corresponds either to a directory in the host or to a directory in another container. This is useful for keeping data that will change and needs to persist (such as the data in this MongoDB database).

The WORKDIR directive sets the currently working directory within the image. This will affect other commands issued within the Dockerfile that rely on relative directories. Think of this as an equivalent to $ cd.

The CMD directive is what Docker will execute as the main process in your container. This process will appear as PID 1 instead of a command like **init**, which is typically used to do important OS stuff. If this process exits (depending on configuration), the container itself will also exit. If you'd like to provide arguments, add them to the array, such as ["mongodb", "--verbose"].

The EXPOSE directives tell Docker which ports you plan on listening for connections from. It's common practice to have an image listen on the *default* port, such as 80 for HTTP or 6379 for Redis. When the container is later executed, there are command-line arguments to specify how those ports will be accessed externally. In the case of MongoDB, two ports are used; one port is for connecting to the database, and the other is for administration.

Another popular directive is ENV, which is used for setting environment variables. The syntax is ENV KEY=value (with quotes required around the value if it contains whitespace).

Not only does Docker perform caching on a per-layer basis (the FROM fields), but it also performs caching on a per-line basis. Each line is read, and the result is cached, so put lines that are likely to change frequently near the end of the file.

For a complete overview of the different Dockerfile directives, including more details and many directives not covered here, check out the Dockerfile reference [24].

Running a Docker Image

If you haven't installed Docker by now, please do so following the installation guide [25] for your platform. Depending on how you install Docker, you may need to run all of these commands as root (prefix them with sudo).

To ensure you've properly installed Docker, run $ docker info to get some information about the running Docker service (if you get an error about being unable to connect to Docker, now would be a good time to try sudo).

Since you've already looked at the Dockerfile for MongoDB, let's go ahead and install it! The first thing you will want to do is *pull* (download the image and its dependencies) by running the command in Listing 3-2. These images are pulled from Docker Hub, which is a repository of both official and user-contributed Dockerfiles [26].

Listing 3-2. Pull MongoDB

```
$ docker pull library/mongo
```

To confirm, you have the image downloaded, you can view a list of all available images by running the command in Listing 3-3.

Listing 3-3. Listing Docker Images

```
$ docker images
REPOSITORY   TAG      IMAGE ID      CREATED        SIZE
mongo        latest   a3bfb96cf65e  47 hours ago   402 MB
```

Now that the images have been downloaded, you can attempt to run the service with the command in Listing 3-4.

Listing 3-4. Running MongoDB with Docker

```
$ docker run -d -p 27017:27017 -v <db-dir>:/data/db \
  --name mongodb library/mongo
```

The -d flag tells Docker that you want to run the container as a daemon. This forks it to the background (as opposed to displaying STDOUT in your terminal or allowing interaction).

The -p flag tells Docker to map ports in the image to the host OS. This means that the MongoDB instance listening inside the image can be accessed from your host OS.

Ports default to using UDP and listening on all interfaces (0.0.0.0). You can prefix the command with an IP address and follow it with a port type. If you wanted to listen only for UDP messages locally on the host port 1337 mapped to container port 4567, you could use 127.0.0.1:1337:4567/udp. If you're using tools such as Redis and MongoDB, which by default are insecure, and if your host is exposed to the Internet, you should listen only for local connections.

The -v flag is for mounting the data volume to the host OS. This will allow you to persist data on the host when the service dies.

The --name flag is used for providing a name to the instance (otherwise, Docker will generate a random one for you like boring_wozniak).

The final argument is the name of the image you want to run. In this case, it's the library/mongo image you pulled earlier.

You can now run the command in Listing 3-5 to check whether your service is running.

Listing 3-5. Listing Running Instances in Docker

```
$ docker ps
CONTAINER ID      IMAGE             COMMAND
25c446a91c20      library/mongo     "/entrypoint.sh mongo"
CREATED           STATUS            PORTS
3 seconds ago     Up 2 seconds      0.0.0.0:27017->27017/tcp
NAMES
mongodb
```

Of course, simply having MongoDB running isn't that much fun if you can't talk to it. The MongoDB image you downloaded also contains the mongo client binary. Docker is malleable and allows you to execute binaries and keep them attached to your terminal! Let's make a connection using the command in Listing 3-6.

Listing 3-6. Docker Running Interactive MongoDB Client

```
$ docker run -it --rm --link mongodb:mymongo \
  library/mongo bash -c 'mongo --host mymongo'
```

This approach runs another instance of the container and links it to the first one, allowing one container to talk directly to the other. If you happened to have the mongo command installed in your host, you could simply run it and connect via the mapped port.

The -it flags tells Docker to pass input from STDIN into the container, allocating a shell to help with this interaction.

The `--rm` flag tells Docker to remove the instance when you're done. Since you're using this instance to temporarily run commands, it would be annoying to have to manually remove it later.

The `--link` flag lets you define a way for linking two different Docker instances. The pair of items that follow are in the format `<instance-name>:<host-alias>`. In this case, your `mongodb` Docker instance can be accessed at the hostname `mymongo` (Docker writes this lookup in the instance's `/etc/hosts` file).

Finally, you tell Docker which image to run (in this case the same `library/mongo` instance), as well as the command to run (in this case a bash shell), which runs the `mongo` client and connects to the `mymongo` hostname.

Docker has the concept of a *registry*, which is where you can pull and push images from and to. Images have *tags* associated with them, which are commonly used for versioning an image. The default Docker registry is Docker Hub, but an organization can choose to host its own Docker registry. By creating a Docker Hub account, you get to host as many public images or a single private image for free; therefore, an organization will want to either pay or create their own registry.

To get a better understanding of how to use the Docker command-line utility, check out the output from `$ docker --help` as well as `$ docker <subcommand> --help`.

Managing Containers with Kubernetes

Kubernetes [27] is "an open-source system for automating deployment, scaling, and management of containerized applications." It was built by Google based on its experiences building and deploying services. It is an opinionated tool, comes with a load balancer, provides services discovery using Etcd [28], and even provides log aggregation. I typically refer to a tool with many included tools as being "batteries included."

The Kubernetes architecture relies on a master and many slave nodes. Feel free to install Kubernetes [29] on two different machines (virtual or physical will be fine). Make sure they're able to communicate with each other over network. These machines will also need to have Docker installed on them.

The master runs on the machine on which you execute `$ kubeadm init`. Once the master has been installed, it will give you a command that you can execute on one of the nodes. The command will be formatted similar to what you see in Listing 3-7.

Listing 3-7. Join Kubernetes Cluster

```
$ kubeadm join --token=000000.ffffffffffffffff 11.22.33.44
```

This command contains a secure token to prevent any bad actors from attempting to join your Kubernetes cluster. Go ahead and run this command on the machine that you want to become a Kubernetes node, and it should join the cluster (if you're feeling daring, you can run this command on multiple machines).

Back on the master machine, you can instruct Kubernetes to run a Docker image for you. The master will look at all the nodes registered to it and determine which one to run the image on. The `run` command has many options, with some translating to Docker counterparts (such as `--port` to specify the port to listen on) and others being used strictly by Kubernetes (such as `--replicas` indicating how many instances to run).

Listing 3-8 shows an example command that comes with the Kubernetes documentation. Behind the scenes this command is interacting with a RESTful API on the Kubernetes master.

Listing 3-8. Calculating Pi with Kubernetes

```
$ kubectl run pi --schedule="0/5 * * * ?" \
  --image=perl --restart=OnFailure \
  -- perl -Mbignum=bpi -wle 'print bpi(2000)'
```

The first argument to the command is a name for the running task, in this case simply `pi`.

The `--schedule` flag instructs Kubernetes to run the task according to the Crontab syntax [30]. In this case, you run the command every five minutes. The syntax is powerful and allows you to do things such as run every Tuesday at noon or the 4th of every month.

The `--image` flag specifies which Docker image to run. Kubernetes is nice enough to download the image if it hasn't already been downloaded. In this case, I'm using the official Perl image.

The `--restart` flag describes the restart policy of this task; you can choose between `Always`, `OnFailure`, and `Never`.

Once the flags have all been set, you can override the Docker command executed for the container. This probably isn't too useful for when you are executing images you've built specifically for your application, but it's useful for this example app. In this case, you use Perl to calculate 2,000 digits of pi.

Executing this command sends the work off to one of the Kubernetes nodes for processing. While the work is being performed, you can query Kubernetes with the command in Listing 3-9 to get a list of the tasks Kubernetes is aware of.

Listing 3-9. Listing Tasks in Kubernetes

```
$ kubectl get pods --all-namespaces
NAMESPACE NAME       READY STATUS           RESTARTS AGE
default   pi-0w1qj 0/1   ContainerCreating 0        3s
```

Further Reading: Mesos and Marathon

You can use many tools in the container orchestration and scheduling space. The most notable one of them is Apache Mesos of which many other tools are based upon.

Apache Mesos [31] "abstracts CPU, memory, storage, and other compute resources away from machines (physical or virtual), enabling fault-tolerant and elastic distributed systems to easily be built and run effectively."

It is probably the most powerful tool for managing containers. It is used for scaling upward of 10,000 containers within some organizations. Containers can be sent to machines based on the RAM and CPU requirements of the containerized app and based on the resources provided by said machine.

Mesos is usually paired with a framework that is used for actually deciding which services need to run in Mesos, how many of them need to run, and so on.

Marathon [32] by Mesosphere is "a container orchestration platform for Mesos and DC/OS." It sits on top of Mesos and adds additional functionality. It can be used for managing other Mesos Frameworks as well.

Marathon provides a RESTful API for performing many actions such as starting a service, scaling it up and down, and destroying the service.

Build Pipeline

The build pipeline is your team's way of representing the flow of code (and other assets) as it makes its journey from being a merged pull request all the way to being deployed to a production environment. In this section, you'll examine some philosophy, how to organize your different environments, and look at tools you can use for running the pipeline.

Continuous Integration and Deployment

First let's dive into some philosophy. One of the greatest advantages of microservices is that each service can be owned by a separate team. Assuming there are enough contracts in place regarding the behavior of a service and tests in place to ensure those contracts are met, then these teams can work autonomously to decide when new features or upgrades can be deployed to production.

With the traditional waterfall approach to releasing software, a team will wait until many features have been completed before deciding to deploy them all at once. With this approach there may be functional bugs in the software that weren't caught ahead of time or perhaps an issue that happens only in production settings. In these cases, you've potentially burned weeks of time of which you could have found and fixed the bug. The engineer who worked on the buggy feature has already moved to another feature and lost all context of the first.

With this in mind, wouldn't it be great if you could merge your changes into a master branch and deploy a feature as soon as it is complete and still be confident that you're not breaking the product? That's exactly what continuous integration (CI) and continuous deployment (CD) promises.

A common CI workflow is that you first write the code required to implement a feature or fix a bug, with tests included, and create a single Pull Request (PR) representing this change. Build software can then examine this PR, run the tests, check for code coverage, and determine whether the PR is acceptable. A human can then check the code for stylish and complexity sake and then fail or merge the PR. Once the PR is merged, you transition into the CD portion. The same build software can take the code, deploy it to testing environments, run some integration tests, and, once confident, deploy the changes to production.

Choosing Environments

Choosing which environments to support is largely dependent on the complexity of your organization as well as how devastating it is if a bug is introduced to production. All corporate projects I've worked on require that the applications be aware of their environment to some extent. Passing in the name of the environment via an environment variable is the typical approach.

At a minimum, your organization should at least support three environments: Development, Staging, and Production.

The Development environment is used when you're doing development on your local machine. Perhaps you crank the level of logging all the way up to 11, filling your terminal with a myriad of debugging information while also disabling outbound logging.

■ **Note** You can take two common approaches when choosing which other services your dev instance will communicate with. One is to configure the discovery service (mentioned later) to talk to a certain other environment (e.g., Staging). Another approach is to run all the services your service needs locally, perhaps by using a tool such as Docker Compose [33].

The Production environment is exactly what it sounds like; it's a production location for your code to run that is accessible by end users. In this situation, you want to log a certain threshold of messages based on importance. You want to communicate with real databases. You're going to be responding to health checks and ideally not crashing as much.

The Staging environment is meant to be an exact replica of Production. When properly maintained, any code running in this environment will behave exactly like it would in the Production environment. Your organization should schedule tasks (e.g., nightly) to copy data from Production to Staging (zeroing out or otherwise anonymizing sensitive customer data if applicable) to keep this environment an accurate depiction of Production.

These three environments represent a *minimum* that your organization should support. If your organization is in a highly regulated industry, such as healthcare or financial, more environments may be needed. I once worked at a financial organization, and it essentially had three distinct staging environments. Overall, it supported Dev, Alpha, Beta, Staging, and Prod. (This organization didn't practice CI and required dedicated teams of QA to merge code and check behavior in each environment.)

Designing a Build Pipeline

Designing a build pipeline depends on the tests you plan on running and the environments you plan on running in. It's useful to look at the environments your organization needs to support as well as the tests you need to run in each environment when determining which build software to choose.

Figure 3-3 shows an example of a generic build pipeline you may choose to support for a particular service. Most CI build software supports the concepts of stages, represented by the rounded-edge boxes, as well as triggers, represented by the arrows. Stages can usually be represented as shell scripts.

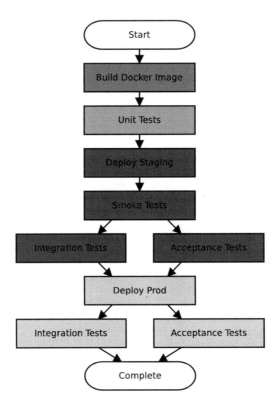

Figure 3-3. *Example of a build pipeline*

The Start box in this diagram represents the time at which you choose to start the build pipeline. This is usually triggered by merging code into the master branch of a code repository. Build tools can usually be configured in one of two ways; either the Git server notifies the build tool of a merge (e.g., with GitHub webhooks) or the build tool can poll the Git server for changes.

After the build process begins, you will first want to build your software. In this case, you're building a Docker container. This stage will run a script inside the directory of a freshly checked-out instance of the codebase, and you will probably be running docker build. Of course, this requires that you package a Dockerfile inside your code repository (usually a good practice).

Once you have a Docker image of your application ready, you will run some basic unit tests. This is a sanity check to make sure you don't deploy broken code to production. Even if your pull requests are running these tests before merging into the master, it's not a bad idea to run them again early in the pipeline. As unit tests shouldn't rely on outside factors, they don't need to run in an "environment." Simply running them on a build server should suffice.

After your unit tests have passed, you will deploy the code to the staging environment. Depending on which tool you use for orchestration, this could mean telling Kubernetes to run. When these deployments happen, you're probably deploying a new version of a service, waiting for it to be healthy, telling whatever load balancer you're using to use the new services, and then tearing down the old ones. You can even configure Kubernetes to perform a "rolling update," deploying new instances and shutting down old instances one at a time.

Next you run some smoke tests. You run these tests before other tests because they should be fast and will give you confidence that other dependent services are also alive. If you didn't run these tests, you may waste time debugging a situation only to realize the problem isn't your fault.

Next you run two tests in parallel, the integration tests and acceptance tests. Build tools usually allow you to specify a stage that needs to complete before triggering the next, and in this case both of those tests run after the smoke tests.

Once those tests have completed and succeeded, you will deploy to production. Build tools should allow you to specify multiple tasks to wait for before beginning a new task. In this case, once the slowest of the two tasks complete, you will deploy to production.

Finally, you run your tests against the production codebase. This is important because if the tests are failing, it may mean that your code is bad (even though staging passed). If tests fail at this point, you will probably want to deploy the previous version of the codebase (known as a *rollback*) so that you can minimize downtime and start fixing the issue.

The more complex a build pipeline is, the more chances a stage can result in failure. A properly configured build pipeline will prevent a product from breaking if a deployment fails (e.g., the whole thing deploys or it doesn't). Deployments are also usually triggered by human interaction, so they shouldn't happen at night. Essentially, a failure shouldn't trigger an emergency, but you do need to know about it so you can fix it. Consider configuring your build software to alert the team via chat as each stage passes or fails or by e-mail during failure. It's also not uncommon to have someone "babysit" a deployment, ensuring each step passes and occasionally "jiggling the handle" if a stage fails.

Building with Jenkins

Jenkins [34] is a popular open source tool for managing builds and performing continuous integration. It has a plug-in system with a rich ecosystem. It can, for example, be configured to poll for changes in a Git branch, build the changes into a Docker container, and then deploy the container using Kubernetes. Jenkins is capable of satisfying the requirements of Figure 3-3.

Jenkins allows you to create a definition of the buildfile and check it into your code repository under the file name Jenkinsfile. This file can also be defined using the web interface, but checking it into version control of course has its advantages: you can keep track of changes over time and see who changed what, reverting when necessary.

Using a `Jenkinsfile` isn't the default approach; within Jenkins you'll want to create a new project with the type *multibranch pipeline*. Normally you would create each build step using the Jenkins UI, but with this approach you're able to declare them using this file.

Listing 3-10 shows an example of a `Jenkinsfile` for a simple side project of mine. This takes advantage of a Jenkins plug-in called the Docker Pipeline Plugin [35] to manage interactions with Docker.

Listing 3-10. Example Jenkinsfile

```
node {
  docker.withRegistry('', 'dockerhub-tlhunter') {
    def image

    stage('Build Docker Image') {
      image = docker.build("tlhunter/radar")
    }

    stage('Docker Push') {
      image.push(env.BUILD_NUMBER)
      image.push('latest')
    }

    stage('Restart Service') {
      sh('/usr/bin/sudo /usr/sbin/service radar restart')
    }
  }
}
```

The syntax used in a `Jenkinsfile` is known as Groovy. Let's take a look at the different calls being used in this file.

The `node{}` block allocates a Jenkins node for performing work on. Jenkins can control many different nodes and send work to different nodes depending on availability and other criteria such as OS and library availability. A node can run on any OS or even inside of a container.

The `docker.withRegistry()` block configures how the plug-in should connect to a Docker repository. The first parameter is empty, which means to use the default Docker Hub. The second parameter is a Jenkins credential ID.

The `stage()` blocks represent individual stages of work. In this case, there are three. The first one builds a Docker image, the second deploys two versions to Docker Hub (one with a build number and one called `latest`), and the final one restarts a SystemD service, which is used for starting the service when the server boots.

The `docker.build()` call performs a Docker build with the specified name.

The `docker.push()` calls push the changes to Docker Hub. It accepts an argument, which is the version to use. Technically with my setup, since I'm building on the same server that I'm deploying to, I don't need to push the image. It will already be available to the Docker daemon. However, when I one day change this build process to deploy to different machines, the image-building step will already be there.

The sh() call executes a shell command on the server. In this case, I'm telling SystemD to restart a service, which is married to a Docker instance.

Listing 3-11 contains the relevant contents of /etc/sudoers, which allows Jenkins to run the service command using sudo.

Listing 3-11. Example /etc/sudoers File

```
jenkins    ALL = NOPASSWD: /usr/sbin/service
```

Listing 3-12 shows the relevant section of my SystemD unit file.

Listing 3-12. Example SystemD Unit File

```
[Service]
Type=simple
Restart=on-failure
ExecStartPre=-/usr/bin/docker kill radar-server
ExecStartPre=-/usr/bin/docker rm radar-server
ExecStartPre=/usr/bin/docker pull tlhunter/radar:latest
ExecStart=/usr/bin/docker run --name radar-server \
  tlhunter/radar:latest
ExecStop=-/usr/bin/docker stop radar-server
```

Figure 3-4 shows the stages and the time each takes to complete for this example.

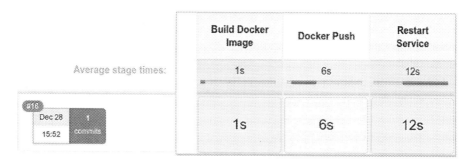

Figure 3-4. *Jenkins build stages*

Of course, for a more complex system, you'll want to use a more complex Jenkinsfile. This one isn't handling testing or sending messages to a container orchestration service. This approach also has several seconds of downtime during a deployment.

The Jenkinsfile has many more configuration options than what is mentioned here. Check out the Jenkins article on the Jenkinsfile [36] for more information.

Testing Contributions

Performing automated testing of code contributions allows you to easily and quickly ensure such contributions meet your expectations before merging. If you require developers to manually check out contributions and manually run tests, it won't be long before laziness kicks in and contributions are merged without being checked.

Build tools that your organization hosts, such as Jenkins, can be configured to keep an eye on pull requests in version management software and then run their tests.

Jenkins

Thanks to the GitHub Pull Request Builder Plugin, you can configure Jenkins to check your project for PRs and then run automated testing against them [37]. Install this plug-in and go through the necessary configuration steps. This will require that you create a new Jenkins project for running the pull requests. You will also want to add either your GitHub credentials or those of a bot account so that the plug-in can authenticate as a user.

Figure 3-5 shows a successfully built pull request for a project of mine. Notice how the user who ran the checks is the same as my user account. The details link in the PR will lead you to the Jenkins build result page for this particular PR.

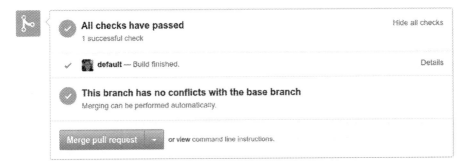

Figure 3-5. A passing Jenkins PR

By default Jenkins is configured to check the project for a pull request every five minutes. This value can be tweaked and even configured via GitHub webhooks so that GH will tell Jenkins when a PR is available.

Travis CI

Travis CI [38] is a tool that is popular for performing continuous integration testing in the open source community (it's free for open source projects). If your project is hosted on GitHub, then configuring your project is easy. Go to the Travis web site, log in with GitHub, accept the OAuth screens, and select your project. You will need to create a file in the root of your project explaining to Travis how your project works.

Listing 3-13 shows an example .travis.yml configuration file, which I use for a project of mine. For my project, I'm instructing Travis that it uses JavaScript (e.g., requires Node.js) and that it uses a typical installation and test command used in the Node.js ecosystem.

Listing 3-13. Example .travis.yml

```
language:
  - javascript
install:
  - npm install
script:
  - npm test
```

With the default configuration, GitHub will tell Travis CI when a pull request has been made that is able to be merged into the main branch. Travis CI will then spin up a container on its servers and run the commands described in the configuration file. Assuming each of the commands exits successfully, the pull request will be considered a pass. Figure 3-6 shows Travis CI failing a bad pull request.

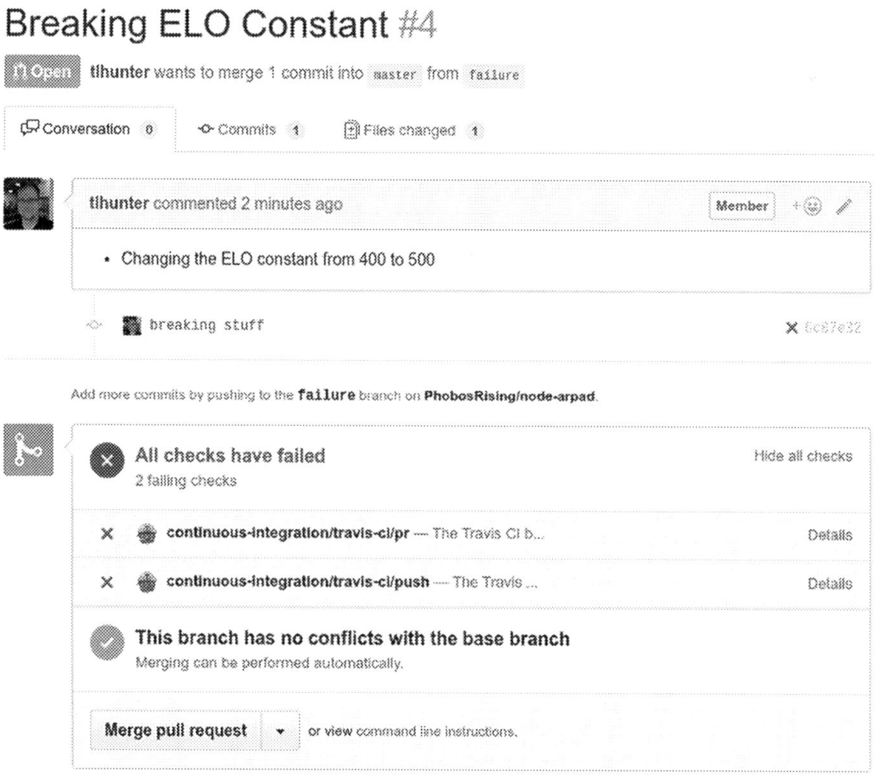

Figure 3-6. *Travis CI GitHub integration*

71

Further Reading: TeamCity and CircleCI

There is no shortage of tools available for managing your build pipeline. Here's a look at some other tools your organization should consider:

- TeamCity [39] is an on-premise paid solution for handling software building and CI, making it really similar to Jenkins. TeamCity is a little easier to learn, and the interface is a little more polished, but you're going to lose out on the large open source community behind Jenkins.

- CircleCI [40] is primarily a software as a solution (SaaS) tool you can use but also offers an on-premise enterprise solution. It is tightly coupled with GitHub, which is good if you host your code there. Integrations are easy to set up, and you won't need to maintain your own on-premise software.

CHAPTER 4

Service Discovery

Service discovery is the process of taking the name of a service as an input and getting a network location of an instance of that service as an output. Discovery is the backbone of any organization practicing highly available microservices.

To achieve high availability, you need to run many instances of each microservice. Ideally, you scale the number of services as load increases, and you're always running a few spares in case an instance fails or there's an unanticipated spike in traffic. Instances need to be able to find and communicate with other instances, and managing all these instances by hand would be a nightmare.

Why Do You Need Service Discovery?

You'll usually want to run a dynamic number of instances on any given machine (virtual or otherwise) for efficiently using random access memory (RAM)/central processing unit (CPU) power, so simply referring to an instance by the hostname isn't enough; you need to use a port number as well.

Discovery is a vital component of any microservice-based system. It needs to be highly available with redundant nodes communicating with one other; otherwise, it becomes a single point of failure. Most popular discovery tools implement a mechanism for performing leader election in case an instance fails. Keep this in mind when selecting a discovery solution.

A given instance in your system can be a consumer of one or more services, a provider of usually one service (microservices should be single purpose), or any such combination. Consumers will need to keep a list of services known to the discovery service and continuously poll for changes or even be pushed changes from the discovery service. Providers need to go through some additional fanfare by registering themselves with the discovery service and repeatedly passing health checks. Figure 4-1 shows how related or unrelated service instances can be assigned to multiple hosts.

© Thomas Hunter II 2017
T. Hunter II, *Advanced Microservices*, DOI 10.1007/978-1-4842-2887-6_4

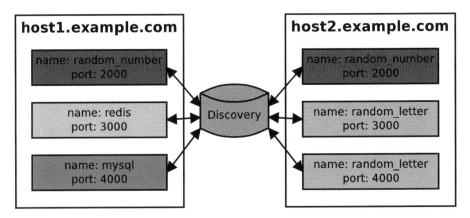

Figure 4-1. *Discovering services on different hosts*

When consumers want to send a request to a provider, assuming they have a cached list of all providers, they can choose which one to send a request to. If the discovery service keeps track of the load of each provider via metadata, it may be possible to know which one is using the least resources and send a query there. More commonly, though, consumers will either implement round-robin, where they cycle through each known instance one at a time, or even simpler choose one of the services at random.

In the perfect scenario there wouldn't need to be a single service address hard-coded into your application, except perhaps for the discovery service itself. Even then there are ways to get around hard-coding potentially a single point of failure, such as giving clients a list of multiple discovery hosts they can connect to in case one is down.

Resiliency and high availability are important features of a discovery tool because they're such an important component within a microservice-practicing organization. Most of these systems are built to allow multiple discovery servers to run and communicate with each other. They will typically implement a quorum, requiring more than half of the servers to agree on the state of data. It's typical for servers to run in groups of three to five so that if one or two were to fail, the system would still function.

One tool worth mentioning is ChaosMonkey, which is a project by Netflix that randomly kills services in a system. Killing services has a desirable side effect of forcing developers to naturally build fault-tolerant systems.

Client Side vs. Server Side

There are two approaches for performing routing requests with service discovery. The first is a client-side approach, and the second is, of course, a server-side approach.

The difference between the two depends on the complexity of determining which service instance to talk to. If the routing complexity lies in the consumer, then the approach is on the client side, and if it lies outside of the client, it is on the server side.

Certainly there are situations where one approach is better than the other, and in my opinion an organization should implement both for different areas of their system.

Client-Side Discovery

This approach involves the least number of network hops from when a request is first sent and data is retrieved and delivered to the initiator. Network latency is frequently one of the largest bottlenecks, so adopting this approach within an organization will result in quicker response times. Figure 4-2 shows client-side discovery.

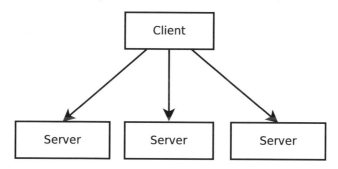

Figure 4-2. *Client-side discovery*

Unfortunately, this approach requires each client to be aware of where the different servers are as well as understand the logic for routing requests between them. Maintaining this list within clients usually requires some sort of asynchronous polling of a database containing server locations. Of course, libraries can be made and shared among clients, but if your organization uses many languages, then many libraries will have to be made.

Server-Side Discovery

This approach involves an additional network hop. This added hop is a centralized location for keeping track of routing information. Figure 4-3 shows server-side discovery.

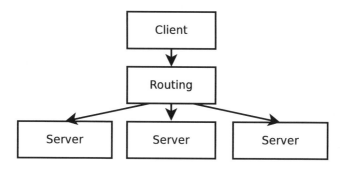

Figure 4-3. *Server-side discovery*

This approach is useful in situations where either clients are incapable of doing routing or you don't want clients to do the routing (for example, the client is external to the organization). Overall system complexity can often be reduced. This approach can introduce a single point of failure depending on how you architect it.

Example Implementation

Let's build a rudimentary discovery server and client from scratch. (However, note that building your own discovery server for use in production is almost always the wrong answer.) This will give you an appreciation for how other tools work. I'll describe several endpoints and their function, and you can implement it.

Feel free to implement this in whatever language you prefer or follow along with the sample implementation I've built for this book [41].

Assumptions: This example implementation will work only with Hypertext Transfer Protocol (HTTP). The server will continuously make HTTP requests to instances at http://host:port/health and expect a 2XX response; if you anything else, you can assume the service is dead. This approach will route requests using client-side discovery.

Get Entire State

When services first launch, they will want to get the entire state of services that the discovery service knows about. This endpoint will also be used for getting periodic updates while polling.

Realistically a discovery consumer may care only about a subset of services inside the discovery service, so a more advanced implementation should allow for filtering. Also, when getting periodic updates, it wouldn't make sense to send the entire list each time; you would want to send just a diff of entries changed since the last poll. However, for the rudimentary example in Listing 4-1, you'll use this single endpoint for getting the initial state as well as updates.

Listing 4-1. Get Entire Discovery State

```
GET /services

{
  "web": [
    {
      "id": "deadbeef",
      "host": "127.0.0.1",
      "port": 20000
    }
  ]
}
```

Register Provider Instance

When a new instance of a discovery provider comes online, it will need to register itself with the discovery service. The endpoint in Listing 4-2 will allow your providers to do just that.

The name of the service is provided in the URL for RESTful purposes, while the location of the service is provided in the body. When you register your service, you also need a special ID to reference your service. This discovery ID will be useful for later deregistering the service.

Listing 4-2. Register Provider Instance to Discovery

```
POST /services/{service_name}

{
  "host": "127.0.0.1",
  "port": 20001
}

{
  "id": "d34db33f",
  "host": "127.0.0.1",
  "port": 20001
}
```

Deregister Provider Instance

If a provider were to stop responding to health checks, it would automatically be removed from the discovery service. Unfortunately, the provider will still be listed in the discovery service for potentially several seconds until the next health check occurs, meaning your providers will get failed requests. You will have your providers manually deregister themselves before exiting to prevent this from happening. Listing 4-3 shows an example of this.

Of course, providers can't always deregister themselves (e.g., if they were killed via crash and don't get a chance). In these cases, consumers will need to implement their own error handling and retry logic.

Listing 4-3. Deregister Provider Instance from Discovery

```
DELETE /services/{service_name}/{instance}

{
  "id": "d34db33f",
  "host": "127.0.0.1",
  "port": 20001
}
```

Finding a Provider

Consumers will need to keep an up-to-date list of providers. There are a few approaches to this, each with their pros and cons.

Consumers Poll Discovery at Intervals

Client-side: This is the approach used in the chapter's example. It is the most rudimentary of the approaches. Each consumer will make requests to the discovery service at a regular interval of ten seconds, each time caching a list of providers and their locations.

The obvious drawback of this approach is that the list will be an average of five seconds outdated. Unless your organization represents a project with the most minimal of traffic and the smallest occurrence of disappearing services, this solution would not be acceptable.

Discovery Tells Consumers via Socket

Client-side: Consumers don't want to go through the pain of registering themselves with the discovery service, and discovery doesn't want to maintain a list of all consumers, so a more ephemeral solution is better. Consumers can open a socket connection with the discovery service (perhaps a long-polling HTTP connection) and continuously get an up-to-date list of changes.

This may be harder to scale from a discovery point of view because maintaining all of these open connections isn't free. It does have the benefit of providing consumers with recent data, perhaps only as latent as tens of milliseconds (whatever the network latency is).

If taking this approach with long-polling HTTP, then a numeric token needs to be generated on the server that is passed to the client. This token increments every time a change happens. This token is required because changes may happen between the time it takes a client to receive updates and to close and reopen another long-polling connection. By passing the token with the new connection, any missed updates can be provided to the client immediately.

Prefix Every Request with a Discovery Lookup

Hybrid: The logic for routing is probably in the consumer, though a discovery endpoint could be constructed that responds with a single recommended provider instance.

In this route, a consumer can ask the discovery service for a list of potential services before every single outbound request, choosing one of the instances to request. Of course, this doubles the amount of outbound requests, slowing down the speed of the consumer.

This approach is beneficial only for one-off tasks, utility scripts, maintenance jobs, and so on. Taking this approach with a frequently used endpoint in your application would be a poor choice.

Use Discovery as a Proxy

Server-side: The logic for routing is in the discovery service, making this noninvasive for clients because they don't need to maintain any lists; they simply make outbound requests. The discovery service will then forward the requests to an appropriate provider and return the results to the consumer.

Later in the "HTTP Routing with Consul" section of this chapter you'll examine a combination of tools that can do just this. I recommend against using it for service-to-service communication because it can add network latency that you won't incur if communicating more directly.

Periodic Health Checks in Provider

There are two popular approaches to performing periodic health checks for discovery. The first method has the providers actively send a message to the centralized discovery service. The second method has the discovery service send requests to the providers.

Discovery Polls Providers

This is the approach used in the chapter's example. In this approach, the central discovery service will send requests to the providers. This may be desirable in situations where providers can't easily make outbound requests. For example, PHP-based applications served behind a web server typically don't have long-running processes; they simply respond to HTTP requests when asked.

A shortcoming to this approach is that a centralized discovery service may get overwhelmed with the task of making so many outbound requests. Also, if providers frequently disappear, then a lot of failed health lookups will be wasted.

Providers Poll Discovery

In this approach, a provider actively sends messages at a regular interval to the discovery service. The discovery service keeps track of the last time requests were received and considers a provider to be gone if a certain time threshold has been met.

This approach can be easier to scale from the point of view of the discovery service. Unfortunately, this is a bit more invasive by requiring providers to schedule asynchronous outbound requests and isn't always an option for certain platforms.

Application Discovery with Consul

Now that you've built a simple application discovery server and have a solid understanding of how to leverage it, let's take a look at a real discovery tool, Consul [42].

You can use Consul in two ways for discovering services. One is on the client side and similar to the system you just built, which makes use of HTTP endpoints to get the state of the system and for updating the state. It also has a second server-side mode where you can use Consul as a Domain Name System (DNS) service, which allows for a less obtrusive method of performing service lookup.

In the "Example Implementation" section of this chapter, I covered many of the different approaches you can choose while designing a discovery system. For example, you can have discovery check the services or have the services report to discovery, you can have services poll for changes or have discovery push changes, and so on. Consul literally supports each of these contrasting solutions and then some, making it a powerful and flexible tool to perform service discovery within your organization.

Registering a Service Instance

In this example, you'll require that your providers send a heartbeat to Consul to let it know that they are healthy, acting as a sort of dead-man's switch. When you register with Consul, you simultaneously register a check in the payload, as shown in Listing 4-4. Consul also allows checks to be added and removed dynamically or even with configuration files, but you won't be examining those methods here.

You use the Check attribute passed during registration to define these checks. Consul supports multiple types of checks such as making outgoing HTTP requests, making Transmission Control Protocol (TCP) connections, and even running shell scripts and examining the return code. Here you're going to use a TTL value of 20s to say the service needs to check in within 20 seconds.

You make use of the Name attribute to tell Consul what type of provider it is, in this case mailer. Later when someone wants to consume the provider, they can ask for mailer and be given an instance. The ID field is equivalent to the discovery ID you built earlier and is used for later deregistering your service and passing health checks.

The Port and Address fields should be familiar as well and are used for constructing requests to your service.

Listing 4-4. Registering an Instance with Consul

```
PUT /agent/service/register

{
    "Name": "mailer",
    "ID": "5da190cf-146d-4f0a-a7a0-73bd64fae187",
    "Address": "localhost",
    "Port": 40002,
    "Check": {
    "TTL": "20s",
    "DeregisterCriticalServiceAfter": "1m"
  }
}
```

Passing a Health Check

Once your application is up and running, you need to send it periodic heartbeats to signal that it is alive. With a TTL value of 20 seconds, you should plan on sending a message even earlier than that, perhaps every 10 seconds. Of course, a higher TTL value means more time can pass before a dead application can be removed from the system. A short TTL value can mean you're sending too much data over the network or can overwhelm Consul. Tweak this value to something you're comfortable with.

When generating a check dynamically, you are able to provide an ID. There's a bit of a "gotcha" when generating a check when registering your application in that you need to prefix the ID of your service with `service:` and use that as the ID of the health check. In this case, the ID you need to use is shown in Listing 4-5.

Listing 4-5. Consul Health Check ID

```
service:5da190cf-146d-4f0a-a7a0-73bd64fae187
```

Finally, you set up an asynchronous task to generate the heartbeats periodically from within your application by making the request shown in Listing 4-6.

Listing 4-6. Consul Heartbeat Request

```
GET /agent/check/pass/service:{service_id}
```

If your application is built using a "sleeping" language such as PHP, you would be better off having Consul query your application with an HTTP check.

Deregistering a Service Instance

Deregistering couldn't be easier; simply make a GET request to a URL and pass in the identifier of your instance. Make the request shown in Listing 4-7 when your application receives a signal to exit.

Listing 4-7. Deregistering with Consul

```
GET /agent/service/deregister/{service_id}
```

Please ignore the RESTful atrocities being committed here.

Subscribing to Updates

Consul supports a feature called *watch* that can be applied to many of the endpoints it supports. These are "blocking" (long-polling) requests that will wait until data has changed before replying with new data. Responses to the client will include a header with an index number, which can then be provided in future requests. These numbers are essentially cursors for keeping track of where you left off.

With the request in Listing 4-8, you make an initial request to Consul asking for a list of healthy instances of a particular service type. The response contains a header named X-Consul-Index.

Listing 4-8. Watching for Updates with Consul

```
GET /v1/health/service/{service_name}?passing=true

X-Consul-Index: 100
```

You are provided with a large amount of information about each of the healthy instances. Listing 4-9 shows an example of a truncated response.

Listing 4-9. Consul Health Update Response

```
[
  {
    "Node": {
      ...
    },
    "Service": {
      "ID": "5da190cf-146d-4f0a-a7a0-73bd64fae187",
      "Service": "mailer",
      "Address": "pluto",
      "Port": 40002,
      ...
    },
    "Checks": [
      ...
      {
        "Node": "pluto",
        "CheckID": "service:5da190cf-146d-4f0a-a7a0-73bd64fae187",
        "Name": "Service 'mailer' check",
        "Status": "passing",
        "ServiceID": "5da190cf-146d-4f0a-a7a0-73bd64fae187",
        "ServiceName": "mailer",
        ...
      }
    ]
  }
]
```

Now that you have this value, you can then make another request to the service. This one will remain open until a change happens. Listing 4-10 shows this request with an increased ID.

Listing 4-10. Watching for More Updates with Consul

```
GET /v1/health/service/{service_name}?passing=true&index=100

X-Consul-Index: 101
```

Each time you get new data, you can replace your in-memory list of running instances and their locations.

HTTP Routing with Consul

Chances are you're making use of a battle-tested web server to handle requests originating from a user outside of your origin, such as Nginx [43], HAProxy [44], or Apache. It's typically not advisable to have a service listening directly for requests from the outside world.

One of the reasons you want a web server between you and your users is that it can perform useful tasks you don't want to bake into the application logic such as TLS termination and Gzip compression. Web servers are also good at tasks such as queueing up HTTP requests and logging basic request information to disk. A web server can even clean up malformed HTTP packets for you.

Limitations of Common Web Servers

Let's examine some limitations of common web servers. Most web services require hard-coded lookups of hostnames/IP addresses to pass HTTP requests to other services.

Nginx Static Configuration

Listing 4-11 shows an example of how to perform simple static round-robin requests with Nginx.

Listing 4-11. Nginx Static Round-Robin Config

```
http {
  upstream service1 {
    server server1.example.com:2001;
    server server1.example.com:2002;
    server server2.example.com:2001;
  }

  server {
    listen 0.0.0.0:80;

    location / {
      proxy_pass http://service1;
    }
  }
}
```

HAProxy Configuration

Listing 4-12 shows how to do that same static round-robin request with HAProxy.

Listing 4-12. Nginx Static Round-Robin Config

```
frontend http-in
  bind 0.0.0.0:80
  default_backend service1

backend service1
  server s1 server1.example.com:2001
  server s2 server1.example.com:2002
  server s3 server3.example.com:2001
```

When you have an architecture with a variable number of services that need to be reached and found via discovery, it becomes tricky to use this with most web servers.

Consul, Consul Template, HAProxy

Luckily, there's a stack of open source technologies you can use to get dynamic routing for incoming HTTP requests. This stack makes use of a project called Consul Template [45], which can be used to reconfigure and restart a web server. If you'd like a hands-on demo of this, check out the demo project that was created for this book [46].

Figure 4-4 gives an overview of a system that allows for a dynamic number of both web services and deeper-level services, all of which are announcing to discovery and with HAProxy properly routing between healthy web services.

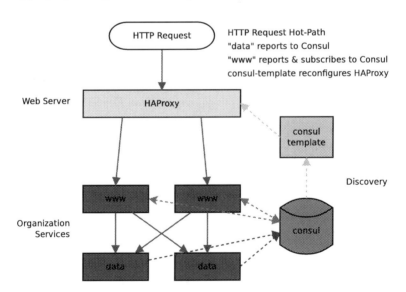

Figure 4-4. *Application discovery with Consul*

HAProxy Template Using Consul Template

Listing 4-13 shows an example configuration file using the syntax required for Consul Template with the intent of generating an HAProxy configuration.

Listing 4-13. advanced.cfg.template

```
frontend http-in
  bind 0.0.0.0:80
  default_backend www

backend www{{range service "www"}}
  server {{.ID}} {{.Address}}:{{.Port}}{{end}}
```

Notice how this configuration is essentially the same as the static configuration.

Compiled HAProxy Configuration

Assuming you have two instances of the www service running and that they're both healthy in Consul, Listing 4-14 shows an example of the generated output.

Listing 4-14. advanced.cfg

```
frontend http-in
  bind 0.0.0.0:80
  default_backend www

backend www
  server service1 host1:30001
  server service2 host2:30002
```

As you can imagine, you could use this same syntax to rewrite the configuration of Nginx.

Consul-Template Command

Listing 4-15 will start an instance of Consul Template, which is configured to read from the configuration template file and write to the configuration file. Once the configuration has been updated, it will run your restart script. Consul Template is smart enough to not run your restart script if the file is the same. This means that if a service other than www changes, it will not trigger a restart.

Listing 4-15. Consul-Template Command

```
$ consul-template -template \
  "./advanced.cfg.template:./advanced.cfg:./restart.sh"
```

HAProxy Restart Script

The reload script in Listing 4-16 will read the newly created `advanced.cfg` configuration written by Consul Template. There are a few important flags that you'll use to start HAProxy. The -p flag tells HAProxy to write its process ID to a file. The -D flag tells HAProxy to daemonize in the background.

Finally, the -st flag tells HAProxy to terminate the process with the given PID (which you read from the `haproxy.pid` file). Something special happens in the background here where the new HAProxy will attempt to take over the previous socket from the old one without dropping any connections. Unfortunately, there is no guarantee that no connections will be dropped.

If you were using Consul Template to restart an Nginx service, you would want to write the configuration file and then restart it like so: `$ nginx -s reload`. This reconfigures Nginx without a restart and shouldn't drop any connections.

Listing 4-16. restart.sh

```
#!/bin/bash

haproxy -f ./advanced.cfg \
  -p ./haproxy.pid -D -st \$(cat ./haproxy.pid)
```

Further Reading

In the quickly evolving world of microservices, there is an ever-growing list of service discovery solutions. The following is a partial list of them with some notes on their functionality.

Apache ZooKeeper and Apache Curator

Apache ZooKeeper [47] is the oldest tool mentioned here. It is used for keeping track of distributed configuration data. By itself it is not a complete service discovery tool. However, when combined with Apache Curator [48], a layer that sits on top of ZooKeeper, you've suddenly got yourself a discovery service.

Both of these tools are written in Java. This approach provides client-side discovery.

Netflix Eureka

Netflix Eureka [49] makes use of client-side routing. Requests are routed round-robin style. It mostly caters to organizations hosted in Amazon Web Services (AWS).

Services are required to send Eureka periodic heartbeats and are removed from the system if they fail.

Eureka is written in Java and has an official Java client. It also provides a RESTful interface for interacting in other languages.

Etcd

Etcd [28] is a tool for distributing key/value data and making this data accessible and consistent. Unfortunately, Etcd doesn't support service discovery out of the box; it needs to be added using a tool such as Registrator.

Etcd is written in Go, and open source client libraries are available in many different languages. It is frequently used as a component of much larger systems such as Kubernets.

Elastic Load Balancer (ELB)

This approach may be the easiest for you if your organization is already locked in to the AWS ecosystem. This approach implements server-side discovery.

Load balancers are the original tool for performing service discovery. A load balancer is essentially a proxy that is aware of multiple service providers. A consumer needs to know only the address of an ELB for the request to be routed appropriately.

CHAPTER 5

Service State

Many services will need to retain state in some form or another. Making your services as "stateless" as possible is something you should strive for. That said, you do need to keep state somewhere, ideally outside of your service instances. This is where databases come into play.

An important rule with databases in relation to microservices is that you don't want to allow any other teams to directly connect to your database. The database should be so far out of reach from your consumers that they shouldn't even know what kind of databases you are using. If a consumer ever does happen upon this information in their day-to-day usage, such as a raw database error being exposed or an architectural shortcoming being exposed, you've introduced some *leaky abstraction*.

The current database landscape is littered with many different types of databases. There are the classical relational database management systems (RDBMSs), typically making use of a Standard Query Language (SQL) dialect. There are also more "modern" concepts such as a document database, typically storing data as JavaScript Object Notation (JSON). Finally, you have access to more specialized types of databases such as very in-memory databases as well as databases that specialize in the ability to loosely search for data based on various criteria.

In this chapter, you'll examine some example database systems in each paradigm by comparing the situations they specialize in, the queries required to get data from them, and the example payloads you can expect in return.

Depending on your service, you may find yourself needing to use two or three different types of databases. While it's true you should strive to use the right tool for the job, try not to stretch yourself too thin. As more databases are introduced, more querying languages need to be learned, and more points of failure can crop up.

Relational Storage with PostgreSQL

PostgreSQL (aka Postgres or PSQL) [50] is an RDBMS that makes use of a SQL dialect for performing queries. An individual record of data (e.g., a user) exists as a row in a table. Attributes of the data (e.g., name, birth date) are called *columns*. Collections of related tables (e.g., tables required for a single project) exist together in a database. A single Postgres instance can have many databases, though you may find in the world of frequently deployed containers that an instance of Postgres will likely contain a single database.

Tables in Postgres require that their columns be defined in advance. Each table column can have different data types, such as numeric or text with variable or predefined lengths. Indexes, which are used for efficiently querying data from a table, also need to be defined ahead of time. The description of the columns and indexes is referred to as a *schema*. Knowing this information before creating and reading records allows for efficiency gains for both performing complex queries and writing data to disk.

All operations done with Postgres can be expressed using SQL queries, everything from the common CRUD operations to more advanced ones such as defining schemas and configuring user permissions. You'll take a look at some example queries, but this book is by no means a manual on Postgres; there are many existing books on this topic.

Later you'll look at an example of a document storage engine, which is useful for storing data expressed as JSON. These types of engines do not require that schemas be defined ahead of time (though some hints can be provided to help indexing run quicker). It is worth noting that Postgres has a column type called JSONB, which does allow for the storage of and fast querying of JSON structured data. This makes Postgres a contender in the world of NoSQL.

Postgres is compliant with the ACID principles [51] of atomicity, consistency, isolation, and durability, and it supports transactions. This means your data isn't going to end up in a bad state if Postgres crashes. Single queries will always run in a way that won't break your data, and more complex queries can be "combined" using transactions so that if any part of the operation fails, then the whole thing fails.

If data stability, transactions, and the ability to work with different types of related data are important for your application, then Postgres may be the right tool for you. RDBMSs are often the go-to solution for important data such as financial or health records.

Postgres requires authentication to connect to it and run queries. By default this is a painful process, requiring user accounts that are integrated into the host operating system (OS). After a bit of configuring, this can be made less painful. When running Postgres inside a Docker container, assuming you're making use of the default image, you can specify credentials when the container is instantiated. Run the commands in Listing 5-1 to get started.

Listing 5-1. Running PostgreSQL with Docker

```
$ mkdir -p ~/data/postgres
$ docker run \
    --name my-postgres \
    -p 5432:5432 \
    -e POSTGRES_PASSWORD=hunter12 \
    -e POSTGRES_USER=zoouser \
    -e POSTGRES_DB=zoodb \
    -v ~/data/postgres:/var/lib/postgresql/data \
    -d postgres
```

Once the server is up and running, you can connect to it using a command-line utility and begin issuing commands. Run the command in Listing 5-2 to connect.

Listing 5-2. Connecting to PostgreSQL via an Interactive Command-Line Interface

```
$ docker run \
    -it --rm \
    --link my-postgres:postgres \
    postgres\
    psql -h postgres -U zoouser zoodb
```

At the prompt you'll want to input the password defined earlier, **hunter12**.

Now let's create some simple tables. Input the SQL from Listing 5-3 into the prompt. These SQL commands are referred to as *schema* when they're used for table creation.

Listing 5-3. Create Table Syntax

```
CREATE TABLE employee (
  Id            SERIAL PRIMARY KEY,
  Username      VARCHAR(32) NOT NULL,
  team_id       INTEGER NOT NULL,
  join_date     DATE NOT NULL
);

CREATE TABLE team (
  id            SERIAL PRIMARY KEY,
  team_name     VARCHAR(64)
);
```

Listing 5-4 creates some sample data so that you have something to work with.

Listing 5-4. Insert Sample Data

```
INSERT INTO team (team_name) VALUES ('Penguin Tamers');
INSERT INTO team (team_name) VALUES ('Lion Tamers');
INSERT INTO team (team_name) VALUES ('Administration');

INSERT INTO employee (username, team_id, join_date)
  VALUES ('tlhunter', 1, '1986-04-01');
INSERT INTO employee (username, team_id, join_date)
  VALUES ('rstyx', 3, '1989-11-05');
```

In Listing 5-3, you specified NOT NULL for each of the fields. Postgres supports the concept of default values. By default if data is not specified during an INSERT, it will default to the special value NULL. Since you've specified NOT NULL, these insert queries would fail if they didn't contain the required data. Notice that you didn't provide values for the id fields; since you've specified them as type SERIAL, Postgres will automatically use an always-incrementing number for you.

Modifying records is pretty simple; you specify the data that you want to change to as well as criteria for which rows to change. Give the query in Listing 5-5 a try.

Listing 5-5. Update Query

```
UPDATE employee SET username = 'steve', team_id = 2 WHERE id = 2;
```

Removing items has a familiar syntax, as you can see in Listing 5-6. Specify which table you'd like to remove rows from as well as the criteria for matching rows.

Listing 5-6. Delete Query

```
DELETE FROM team WHERE id = 3;
```

Now that you've inserted some data and changed it, let's take a look at what's in your database. Issue the command shown in Listing 5-7, and you should see the same output.

Listing 5-7. Select Query and Output

```
SELECT * FROM employee;

id | username  | team_id | join_date
---+-----------+---------+------------
1  | tlhunter  |       1 | 1986-04-01
2  | steve     |       2 | 1989-11-05

SELECT * FROM team;

id | team_name
---+----------------
1  | Penguin Tamers
2  | Lion Tamers
```

At this point, if you wanted, you could query the table for all users on a specific team_id. You can do this using a WHERE clause, as shown in Listing 5-8.

Listing 5-8. Select Query with WHERE Clause

```
SELECT * FROM employee WHERE team_id = 2;

id | username | team_id | joined_date
---+----------+---------+-------------
2  | steve    |       2 | 1989-11-05
4  | bob      |       2 | 2010-05-01
```

Since you're not dealing with a lot of data, the query would be fast. However, if you had thousands of employees, then you might start to notice the query slowing down. The reason for this is Postgres has to slowly look through each entry in the table, matching records that have a team_id of 2. Here's where a powerful feature of SQL comes into play. You can specify that you want an index on the team_id column.

With an index, Postgres will maintain a structure of the team_id's for you in a manner that is efficient to query. This does have some trade-offs, however. Each time you insert data into a table with an index, Postgres will need to update both the row in the table and the index structure. There are also storage costs involved for maintaining that index. In general, you probably want to add an index to columns you will frequently use for querying.

Listing 5-9 shows how you can add an index to your employee table for the team_id column.

Listing 5-9. Create an Index

```
CREATE INDEX ON employee(team_id);
```

Now if you were to run the same select from before, you would receive the employee data faster.

There are many kinds of indexes; you can also create UNIQUE indexes for preventing duplicate entries within a table (such as a username field for logging in). You can also have compound indexes that prevent a table from having duplicates of a pair of data. This would be useful in the case of GitHub where a user can have only one repo with a certain name but different users can have repos sharing a name. You can even have indexes allowing you to do quick full-text searches (which records contain a set of words) as well as spatial (think geolocation) searches.

If you want to cross-reference data between the employee table and the team table with a nonrelational system, this would probably require that you make redundant copies of the data, such as duplicating the team name into each of the employee records. This results in more data on disk as well as complexity when you perform a team rename. Thanks to the power of SQL joins, you can write a query like the one in Listing 5-10.

Listing 5-10. Joining Data from Multiple Tables

```
SELECT employee.*, team.team_name FROM employee
  LEFT JOIN team ON employee.team_id = team.id;
```

```
id | username | team_id | join_date  |  team_name
---+----------+---------+------------+----------------
1  | tlhunter |       1 | 1986-04-01 | Penguin Tamers
2  | steve    |       2 | 1989-11-05 | Lion Tamers
```

I've covered a tiny subset of the capabilities of Postgres. One of the more powerful features is the ability to create foreign key constraints, a feature that can force data consistency between two tables (such as employee.team_id referencing team.id). Consider reading the chapter on Postgres queries on the Postgres documentation web site to get a better understanding of its possibilities.

RETURNING Clause

Postgres has a feature that is useful in the context of microservices. When performing a SELECT operation, you will naturally get the data returned that you've asked for. However, when performing an INSERT, UPDATE, or DELETE, you do not get row data returned.

This means when you perform a non-SELECT operation, you can't get data back, such as an HTTP PUT, which correlates to a Postgres UPDATE. Unfortunately, you would normally have to perform an UPDATE operation immediately followed by a SELECT operation to return the data.

By using the clause RETURNING and then providing a list of columns (or simply using *), you can get the data of the resulting row. This means that when a CREATE is performed with computed properties (i.e., an automatically generated ID or a created datetime), you get the host back as well. Try running the query in Listing 5-11 to see this for yourself.

Listing 5-11. INSERT with RETURNING Clause

```
INSERT INTO employee (username, team_id, joined_date)
 VALUES ('bob', 2, '2010-05-01') RETURNING *;

id | username | team_id | joined_date
---+----------+---------+-------------
4  | bob      |       2 | 2010-05-01
```

Using this feature, you're able to touch the database and return the data to the consumer with a single database operation.

When to Use PostgreSQL

If you have data with attributes that will not change frequently, if you need guarantees that your data will be safe in the event of crashes, or if you don't need the absolute fastest performance, Postgres is the perfect tool for the job. In addition, if your data is spread across collections containing different types of related data that needs to be merged, then Postgres is a good tool.

When Not to Use PostgreSQL

If your data schema is highly volatile and constantly changing, Postgres can get tricky to manage. That said, many object-relational mapping (ORM) tools provide functionality for performing schema migrations (which usually come at the cost of some downtime). If much of the data will end up being sparse, that is to say large amounts of data will not use certain attributes, then a document storage database could be a better bet. If you don't need to perform complex queries, perhaps only grabbing data by an identifier, there are simpler solutions out there.

Further Reading: MySQL

MySQL is the most popular open source SQL database. It will be able to perform similar types of operations as Postgres though with slightly different SQL syntax and performance characteristics.

The MySQL company was purchased by Oracle, and as a result the project was openly forked by the community under the name of MariaDB. The two databases are similar but will likely diverge more over time.

With MySQL being so similar to Postgres, the choice of which one to use really comes down to the following: are the members of your team more familiar with one or the other, and does your organization already have instances of one or the other? Not having to train employees or add operational overhead of supporting another database is important.

Document Storage with MongoDB

MongoDB (aka Mongo) [52] is a database specializing in storing JSON documents (though under the hood they're stored in a binary format called BSON). MongoDB queries are written in the form of specialized JSON objects.

By default Mongo doesn't require authentication to run, which is fine because it listens for only local connections by default. If you ever listen for remote connections, be sure to enable authentication!

Let's install Mongo and run some sample queries to get an understanding of how it works. First run the commands in Listing 5-12 to get started.

Listing 5-12. Running MongoDB with Docker

```
$ mkdir -p ~/data/mongo
$ docker run \
    --name my-mongo \
    -p 27017:27017 \
    -v ~/data/mongo:/data/db \
    -d mongo
```

This will download the necessary Docker images and get the service running. Once it's ready, let's run an interactive Mongo read-evaluate-print loop (REPL) by running the command in Listing 5-13.

Listing 5-13. Run the Interactive Mongo REPL

```
$ docker run \
    -it --rm \
    --link my-mongo:mongo \
    mongo \
    sh -c 'exec mongo --host mongo'
```

The mongo command gives you a JavaScript interface for interacting with Mongo. It allows you to execute the same kind of JSON queries that you would write in your application code as well as some shortcut commands to make the REPL easier to use.

When you run a command in Mongo, you're executing JavaScript methods. Whichever library you choose to use with your application will most likely map the commands you are able to run in the shell to methods you're able to run within your application. This means each of the commands you execute here can directly translate into application code.

Let's create a database called zoo and insert a couple sample record into a collection named cages by running the commands in Listing 5-14. The lines beginning with > are the lines that you will enter as to reflect the behavior of the Mongo REPL.

Listing 5-14. Create Database and Insert Records

```
> use zoo
switched to db zoo
> db.cages.insert({"name": "Penguin Pen", "temperature": 10});
  WriteResult({ "nInserted" : 1 })
> db.cages.insert({"name": "Lion Pen", "temperature": 70});
  WriteResult({ "nInserted" : 1 })
> db.cages.insert({"name": "Pig Pen", "temperature": 60});
  WriteResult({ "nInserted" : 1 })
```

Notice that you receive metadata about the queries after you execute them. This data will be available to you when you execute code within your application as well. Now that you've inserted a record, let's get a list of all records in the cages collection by running the commands in Listing 5-15.

Listing 5-15. Find All Records

```
> db.cages.find()
{
  "_id": ObjectId("58c5ba7f8f4cf57433e4ed60"),
  "name": "Penguin Pen", "temperature": 10
}
{
  "_id": ObjectId("58c5ba898f4cf57433e4ed61"),
  "name": "Lion Pen", "temperature": 70
}
{
  "_id": ObjectId("58c5ba918f4cf57433e4ed62"),
  "name": "Pig Pen", "temperature": 60
}
```

Much like you saw earlier with Postgres, an identifier was automatically created for you. In Mongo's case, the identifier is called _id. Unlike Postgres, however, you didn't need to define a schema or any sort of mechanism to get this primary key; you just get it for free.

Speaking of the _id property, you may be wondering why it's printed weird and why you're seeing ObjectId next to it. Mongo uses a special 12-byte binary type called an ObjectId to represent these default primary keys. This is fine for BSON; however, representing these identifiers in JSON is painful. Whatever module you use to communicate with Mongo will provide a convenient way to deal with them. You can also create your own _id using, say, a string or integer instead.

Mongo uses a unique syntax for querying based on properties. Essentially you run the db.collection.find() method and provide key/value pairs to match attributes in the document. If you are looking for documents with a simple equal comparison (e.g., name equals Pig Pen), simply provide the value. Listing 5-16 has such a query.

Listing 5-16. Find Specific Record

```
> db.cages.find({"name": "Lion Pen"});
{
  "_id": ObjectId("58c5ba898f4cf57433e4ed61"),
  "name": "Lion Pen", "temperature": 70
}
```

Listing 5-17 shows a more advanced query that will search for records where the temperature is greater than ($gt operator) 50 and less than ($lt operator) 65. Notice how you provide a more complex object as the value.

Listing 5-17. Advanced Find Query

```
> db.cages.find({
  temperature: {
    $gt: 50,
    $lt: 65
  }
});
{
  "_id": ObjectId("58c5ba918f4cf57433e4ed62"),
  "name": "Pig Pen", "temperature": 60
}
```

Just like with Postgres, the creation of indexes is vital for allowing faster reading of information. If you know that you wanted to frequently query based on the .temperature field of your documents, you could create the index as described in Listing 5-18.

Listing 5-18. Creating an Index

```
> db.cages.createIndex({"temperature": 1});
{
  "createdCollectionAutomatically": false,
  "numIndexesBefore": 1,
  "numIndexesAfter": 2,
  "ok": 1
}
```

Mongo supports many arithmetic and Boolean operators that resemble their counterparts in most computer languages. To distinguish an operator from a normal attribute, operators will always begin with a dollar sign, $. For a more comprehensive listing, check out the documentation on Mongo operators [53].

When you perform an update to your data, you can use either two or three parameters. The first parameter specifies a query for matching a document with. This is the same query you'd use with the .find() method and is analogous to a WHERE clause in SQL.

The second parameter is a document that will replace the existing document. The third parameter contains additional options, such as .multi to specify if you should affect multiple documents (defaults to false and analogous to a LIMIT 1 clause in SQL).

Let's run the query in Listing 5-19 to turn up the heat for your penguins.

Listing 5-19. Updating Records

```
> db.cages.update({
  "name": "Penguin Pen"
}, {
  "name": "Penguin Pen", "temperature": 20
});
WriteResult({ "nMatched": 1, "nUpserted": 0, "nModified": 1 })
```

Now, if you query the database again using Listing 5-20, you'll find your penguins to be a little warmer.

Listing 5-20. Finding Updating Records

```
> db.cages.find({"name": "Penguin Pen"});
{
  "_id": ObjectId("58c5c1b88f4cf57433e4ed63"), "name": "Penguin Pen",
  "temperature": 20
}
```

If you want to circumvent the default behavior of replacing an entire document, you can use the $set operator like in Listing 5-21. Once present, a document will be only partially updated.

Listing 5-21. Updating a Partial Document

```
> db.cages.update({
  "name": "Penguin Pen"
}, {
  "$set": {
    "temperature": 30
  }
});
WriteResult({ "nMatched" : 1, "nUpserted" : 0, "nModified" : 1 })
```

The .upsert flag on update commands allows you to update an existing record that matches the query syntax, or if one does not already exist, you will create a new one. Run the command in Listing 5-22 to see this for yourself. A variation of this command exists in many database systems. Unfortunately, this operation is not atomic within Mongo; if you run multiple upsert commands in parallel, you may end up with duplicate documents.

Listing 5-22. Performing an Upsert

```
> db.cages.update({
  "name": "Turtle Pen"
}, {
  "name": "Turtle Pen", "temperature": 80
}, {
  "upsert": true
});
WriteResult({ "nMatched" : 0,
  "nUpserted" : 1,
  "nModified" : 0,
  "_id" : ObjectId("58c5c91fe7ef07bbdc82d5ee")
})

> db.cages.update({
  "name": "Turtle Pen"
}, {
  "name": "Turtle Pen", "temperature": 80
}, {
  "upsert": true
});
WriteResult({
  "nMatched" : 1,
  "nUpserted" : 0,
  "nModified" : 1
})
```

To remove entries from Mongo, you can use the .remove() collection method. You provide it first with a query argument, like you used for finding and updating data, and optionally a second argument, configuring removal settings (e.g., .justOne to specify at most one record should be removed, defaults to false). The command in Listing 5-23 shows an example of how to remove a single record.

Unlike .find(), however, you can't leave the first argument empty to catch all items. This is to prevent you from accidentally deleting everything. Provide an empty object if you do want to delete everything.

Listing 5-23. Removing a Record

```
> db.cages.remove({"name": "Lion Pen"});
WriteResult({ "nRemoved" : 1 })
```

When to Use MongoDB

Mongo is a great tool for prototyping. In the early stages of project development, it can be nice to not have to worry about keeping a schema up-to-date. Defaulting to no authentication further makes it easy to stand up for prototyping. If you need to store data that can change a lot per entity, then Mongo may be a better fit than SQL (which would require many NULLs).

When Not to Use MongoDB

Mongo can apply ACID guarantees only on a per-document basis, so it may not be a good fit in situations where you need to guarantee a perfect state of data. If your data always adheres to the same schema, Mongo may not be a good fit (there is additional overhead in storing per-document attribute names as compared to a database column). If there is a required relationship between entities (e.g., you need the ability to "join" different documents), Mongo may not be a good fit (you can nest related entities in a single document, but this has its drawbacks as well).

If you already use Postgres in your organization and want to store queryable schemaless JSON data, it's worth noting that Postgres's JSONB column type supports this as well.

Further Reading: CouchDB

CouchDB is a popular open source alternative to MongoDB. It also stores data in a convenient JSON format.

One thing that makes CouchDB unique is that it keeps versions of old data around. New versions get an incrementing version attribute in the document. This is useful in situations where you want to write a lot and keep old copies of entities around. For example, the wildly popular Node Package Manager (NPM) uses CouchDB as a database. With NPM, users are constantly publishing new versions of packages, while old versions are intended to stick around indefinitely.

Fast Data Structures with Redis

Redis [54] is an amazing tool with a simple interface. At its heart, it is an in-memory key/value store. It is easily configured and can be used to persist data on disk. Redis is so malleable in fact that I'll cover it for numerous situations throughout this chapter. I highly recommend you add Redis to your tool belt.

Redis has a convenient philosophy that makes it easy to work with. Keys do not need to be declared (such as would be required in most programming languages) before they can be operated on. This means if you perform a numeric operation on a key, it will assume 0; if you perform list operations, it will assume an empty list; and so on.

Redis supports two different formats for persisting data on disk. The first format is called RDB and represents a complete snapshot of all the data in Redis in its simplest form. However, this file can be expensive to generate. The other format is called AOF and contains a list of commands required to regenerate the state of Redis. This file can essentially be streamed while Redis runs, though it is much less compact.

You can easily run a Redis Docker instance locally to issue commands and gain familiarity. The commands in Listing 5-24 will create a new instance using the AOF persistence (`--appendonly yes`) and save the content to disk between restarts. It will listen for connections from your machine if you'd like to write code that interacts with it.

Listing 5-24. Running Redis with Docker

```
$ mkdir -p ~/data/redis
$ docker run \
    --name my-redis-db \
    -p 6379:6379 \
    -v ~/data/redis:/data \
    -d redis \
    redis-server --appendonly yes
```

The Redis server is typically configured using a file called `redis.conf` [55]. Luckily for users of Docker, these configuration settings can be overridden by CLI arguments.

Once you have the service running (`redis-server`), you can connect to it using a simple CLI utility (`redis-cli`). This utility comes with the base Redis image and provides some niceties such as command completion. (The protocol used to communicate with Redis is so simple that if you wanted, you could even use a utility like Telnet.) Run the command in Listing 5-25 to connect to your running Redis instance.

Listing 5-25. Connect to Redis via CLI Utility

```
$ docker run \
    -it \
    --link my-redis-db:redis \
    --rm \
    redis \
    redis-cli -h redis -p 6379
```

By default Redis doesn't require any authentication. This sounds a little dangerous, but it also only listens for connections on the local machine by default. If you do configure Redis to listen for external requests, be sure to enable authentication. Authentication can be enabled by setting the `requirepass <password>` configuration and then by executing `AUTH <password>` after a client has connected.

Redis is a key/value store. Each key that is stored in Redis can contain different types of data. These primitive data types are powerful and can be used to model complex use cases in your application.

Data Types

Let's take a look at the types of data that Redis lets you store. You'll also look at some sample commands as well as an example interaction with Redis.

Strings are the most basic type of data that you can store in Redis. Strings can contain binary data (e.g., the contents of a file). Keep in mind that you can serialize a complex object in your application as JSON and store it in Redis, though you can't query against it like with other NoSQL databases.

Common commands used with strings include SET key value for setting a value and GET key for retrieving the value. When storing numeric data in a key, you can perform some basic arithmetic against the value such as with INCR key and DECR key, which will increase and decrease the value. Once you want to get rid of a key, you can remove it with DEL key (which works on any data type). You can see these commands in action in Listing 5-26.

Listing 5-26. Common Redis Commands

```
redis:6379> GET author
(nil)
redis:6379> SET author "Thomas Hunter II"
OK
redis:6379> GET author
"Thomas Hunter II"
redis:6379> DEL author
(integer) 1
redis:6379> DEL author
(integer) 0
```

Lists contain ordered sets of data, typically ordered based on when you insert the data, though there are ways to change the order. This concept is analogous to an array in many computer languages. Items in lists can repeat.

To get the length of a list, you can use LLEN key. To get the elements in a list, you can use LRANGE key start stop, where start is the start of a zero-based list and stop is the end. You can use negative numbers to represent from the end of the list, so -1 represents the last item. LPUSH and RPUSH add items to the beginning and end of the list. LPOP and RPOP remove items from the beginning and end. Listing 5-27 shows an example of these commands.

Listing 5-27. Redis List Commands

```
redis:6379> LLEN friends
(integer) 0
redis:6379> RPUSH friends joe
(integer) 1
redis:6379> RPUSH friends steve jon
(integer) 3
redis:6379> LLEN friends
(integer) 3
redis:6379> RPOP friends
"jon"
redis:6379> LRANGE friends 0 -1
1) "joe"
2) "steve"
```

Hashes contain key/value pairs within the hash. Values need to be strings (e.g., you can't have a list in a hash). Hashes are analogous to the concept of objects in many languages. They are useful for keeping related data together (e.g., data that should be destroyed at the same time).

You can set and get individual hash entries using the HSET key field value and HGET key field value. You can get a list of fields using HKEYS key, and you can count the fields using HLEN key. To get all fields, use HGETALL key, and to remove a field, use HDEL key field. Listing 5-28 shows an example of these commands.

When getting hash data, the CLI tool will display field/value pairs as siblings; however, whichever application library you're using will likely convert them into a native object for convenience.

Listing 5-28. Redis Hash Commands

```
redis:6379> HSET tom age 30
(integer) 1
redis:6379> HSET tom name "Thomas Hunter II"
(integer) 1
redis:6379> HGET tom age
"30"
redis:6379> HGETALL tom
1) "age"
2) "30"
3) "name"
4) "Thomas Hunter II"
```

Sets contain unordered, unique data. Inserting the same item twice will result in it "existing" only once inside the set.

To add entries to a set, use SADD key member. To count the number of entries, use SCARD key (cardinality), or if you want all members, use SMEMBERS key. To tell whether a string is a member, use SISMEMBER key member. To remove an entry, use SREM key member. Listing 5-29 shows an example of these commands.

Listing 5-29. Redis Set Commands

```
redis:6379> SADD hobbies gardening
(integer) 1
redis:6379> SADD hobbies running
(integer) 1
redis:6379> SADD hobbies gardening
(integer) 0
redis:6379> SCARD hobbies
(integer) 2
redis:6379> SISMEMBER hobbies dancing
(integer) 0
```

Sorted sets are a sort of hybrid of hashes and sets. Values need to be unique like a set. However, they are also associated with a numeric score (which doesn't need to be unique). You can then do complex operations on values based on their score values.

The command ZADD key score member can be used to add entries to a set, allowing for multiple score/member pairs to be repeated. ZCARD key will count the number of entries. ZRANGEBYSCORE key min max is a complex command that can get you entries within the specified range and has optional clauses like WITHSCORES to include scores. ZRANK key member will tell you the overall rank of a particular member. ZREM key member will remove a member. Listing 5-30 shows an example of these commands.

Listing 5-30. Redis Sorted Set Commands

```
redis:6379> ZADD highscores 100 thomas 200 jon
(integer) 2
redis:6379> ZADD highscores 110 rupert 90 piccolo
(integer) 2
redis:6379> ZCARD highscores
(integer) 4
redis:6379> ZRANGEBYSCORE highscores 95 115 WITHSCORES
1) "thomas"
2) "100"
3) "rupert"
4) "110"
redis:6379> ZRANK highscores rupert
(integer) 2
```

Geolocation data is actually stored internally using the Sorted Set data type; however, you get special geo commands that you can run against this geolocation data, which makes it worth explaining separately.

GEOADD key longitude latitude member is how you add entries to geolocation. GEODIST key member1 member2 will give you the distance between two members (units default to meters). GEORADIUS key longitude latitude radius will get you all members within a radius of the inputted location and has optional clauses such as WITHCOORD and WITHDIST to return the member's location and distance from center. To remove an entry, you use the same ZREM key member command from sorted sets. Listing 5-31 shows an example of these commands.

Listing 5-31. Redis Geolocation Commands

```
redis:6379> GEOADD city -122.419103 37.777068 san-francisco
(integer) 1
redis:6379> GEOADD city -122.272938 37.807235 oakland
(integer) 1
redis:6379> GEORADIUS city -122.273412 37.869103 10 km
    WITHCOORD WITHDIST
1) 1) "oakland"
   2) "6.8814"
   3) 1) "-122.27293699979782104"
      2) "37.8072354483954669"
```

Atomic Operations with MULTI/EXEC

Let's consider a situation in which you want to build a distributed task scheduler. The goal of this scheduler is to perform simple jobs on one of several service instances. You need to ensure that a task will get executed only once. You can represent tasks using a sorted set where the score of a record is the timestamp in milliseconds. Every second you can have each service instance poll the database for work to perform.

Imagine that two jobs are added to the queue. Job 1 is scheduled for five seconds in the future, and job 2 is scheduled for ten seconds in the future. You can see this happening in Listing 5-32.

Listing 5-32. Adding Jobs to Your Task Scheduler

```
ZADD jobs 1488855734119 "execute job 1"
ZADD jobs 1488855739119 "execute job 2"
```

Next you read jobs from the queue using ZRANGEBYSCORE, which looks for jobs starting at score 0 (the beginning of time) to now (the score is the current timestamp). When you find jobs, you delete them using ZREMRANGEBYSCORE so that no other service instance can claim the same jobs. Your service will execute the two commands shown in Listing 5-33 one after another.

Listing 5-33. Naive Approach for Retrieving Jobs

```
ZRANGEBYSCORE jobs 0 1488855737119
ZREMRANGEBYSCORE jobs 0 1488855737119
```

Unfortunately, there is a race condition in this code! Service instance #1 can perform the read operation, receiving a list of jobs to perform. Immediately afterward, service instance #2 can make the same read command, getting the same list. Once that's done, both servers could end up running the removal command. This would result in both service instances executing the same job.

To fix this, you can have each service instance surround their commands using the MULTI and EXEC commands, as shown in Listing 5-34. This will prevent any service instances from interlacing commands before another set of commands has completed.

Listing 5-34. Better Approach for Retrieving Jobs

```
MULTI
ZRANGEBYSCORE jobs 0 1488855737119
ZREMRANGEBYSCORE jobs 0 1488855737119
EXEC
```

When the MULTI command starts, Redis will queue the commands from the connected client until EXEC is called. Only once the EXEC is called are the commands executed. Other connected clients can still execute commands until the final EXEC call is made, so it isn't locking the entire database. Remember that Redis is single-threaded.

Execute Lua Scripts on Redis Server

The MULTI and EXEC commands are a great way to enforce atomicity in your command execution. Unfortunately, you're unable to "chain" commands together, meaning you can't use the output of an earlier command to affect a later command. If you need to perform any logic, such as read the value of another key based on the value in an earlier key, you would be forced to make multiple calls from your application. Multiple calls would slow down the overall operation.

This is where the EVAL and SCRIPT family of commands come into play. These commands allow you to evaluate Lua scripts on the Redis server. You will specifically look at the situation where you load a script from your application (this is best done early on in the bootstrapping process, meaning when a service instance first starts). When you load a script, you are given the SHA1 hash of the script in return, which you can think of as Redis naming your script for you. You can refer to this hash later to execute the script. Loading the same script over and over has no side effects.

Let's go back to the geolocation example you looked at earlier. In that example, you would get identifiers of cities that were within a specified radius. But imagine you have a separate Redis hash that contains JSON data about each of the cities, keyed by city ID. Instead of executing GEORADIUS from your application and later running HMGET (which stands for "hash multiple get"), let's perform the operations in a single request.

First let's create some data, as shown in Listing 5-35. You'll make use of two keys, the first containing geolocation data and being named city. The second is a hash containing data about cities and is called data.

Listing 5-35. Create Some Geo and Hash Data

```
GEOADD city -122.419103 37.777068 sf
HSET data sf '{"name": "San Francisco", "temp": 65}'

GEOADD city -122.272938 37.807235 oak
HSET data oak '{"name": 'Oakland', "temp": 72}'
```

Now let's create a file called get-cities.lua, shown in Listing 5-36. This file will be read by your application and later be sent to Redis.

Listing 5-36. get-cities.lua

```
-- get-cities.lua: Find cities within 10km of query

local key_geo = KEYS[1]
local key_data = KEYS[2]

local longitude = ARGV[1]
local latitude = ARGV[2]

local city_ids = redis.call(
  'GEORADIUS', key_geo, longitude, latitude, 10, 'km'
)
return redis.call('HMGET', key_data, unpack(city_ids))
```

The double hyphens (--) are used to represent a comment (much like in SQL).

The next lines declare some variables, pulling them from some global argument arrays. One thing to note is that the arrays are 1-based (instead of 0-based like most languages). You have two arrays to get data from. The first is KEYS, which you can use to pass in names of Redis keys you want to interact with. The second is ARGV, which will contain other types of arguments.

You may be wondering why Redis requires two separate arrays for keys and arguments instead of just one. This is because Redis needs a way to declaratively know which keys are being acted upon for each Redis query. Knowing which keys to act upon lets Redis communicate with the correct servers when it runs in cluster mode. This leaves you with a hard requirement to know each key name ahead of time. (Technically if you run with a single Redis instance, you could hard-code key names into the script or dynamically generate them, though this will bite you later when you need to scale.)

The redis.call() calls are how Lua scripts are able to execute Redis commands. The first argument is the name of the Redis command followed by the rest of the command arguments. When you run GEORADIUS, you pass in the name of the key, the location information, and radius information.

In the second call, you run HMGET, passing in the appropriate key, as well as the arguments. This command takes multiple hash field names as separate arguments. The unpack() function takes the array of city IDs you retrieved from the GEORADIUS command and sends them to HMGET as separate arguments. Finally, the result of the HMGET command is returned to the caller.

Now that you know how the script works, let's load it. Pass the contents of the script to Redis (with newlines escaped as n characters), as you can see in Listing 5-37. (Note you'll need to enter it on a single line.)

Listing 5-37. Load the Lua Script

```
SCRIPT LOAD "<script contents>"
```

The result of this command is an SHA1 hash. You can then call the script using the hash with EVALSHA <hash> <key count> <keys> <values> like you see in Listing 5-38. Since the keys and values are normal command arguments, you need to tell Redis how to differentiate the two. That is exactly what the key count argument is for.

Listing 5-38. Execute Lua Script on Redis Server

```
EVALSHA <hash> 2 city data -122.273412 37.869103
```

The result of this command will be an array of JSON objects representing the cities within 10km of Berkeley. In this case, you should just receive the JSON for Oakland.

Caching

You make use of caching so that data that is "expensive" isn't unnecessarily generated multiple times. This can cover many types of data, such as session data, the result of a slow database query, or even the response from a paid external API. With Redis being an in-memory key/value storage and being so quick to query, it is a perfect tool for performing caching.

Redis offers several nice features that are useful with regard to caching. These features usually fall into one of two categories: setting a per-key expiration and enabling a configurable global least recently used (LRU) cache. Both of these features can be used in tandem.

An LRU cache is a generic name for something that holds data and keeps track of the last time each piece of data has been accessed. These caches can hold only a configurable amount of data (ideally less data than the amount of RAM available on the machine). When one of these caches starts to go over the limit, it will then start removing entries that haven't been recently touched.

Redis lets you run it in LRU mode using the maxmemory directive. This configuration takes a number of bytes and a unit, for example, 512mb. Redis will fill memory until it reaches this limit and then remove items after the memory limit has been exceeded. This means it is not a hard limit, so you should set it lower than the actual memory constraint of the machine. Listing 5-39 shows an example of this configuration.

Listing 5-39. Redis LRU Cache Configuration

```
maxmemory 512mb
maxmemory-policy volatile-ttl
```

It is usually accompanied by a second directive, maxmemory-policy, which describes the behavior for evicting keys from memory. There are a few options available for the directive, each option being useful for different situations.

- noeviction: Error when adding data (default)

- allkeys-lru: Evict any key based on last usage

- allkeys-random: Evict any key randomly

- volatile-lru: Evict expirable key based on last usage

- volatile-random: Evict expirable key randomly

- volatile-ttl: Evict a key starting with shortest expiry

The previous volatile options will throw an error when adding an item that would put the memory usage over the limit. Technically it's possible to use the volatile options so that you can use Redis as *both* an LRU cache and a persistent storage assuming you set an expiration on entries you want to use as a cache. In general, though, it's better to have a separate Redis instance for caching versus persistence.

There are a few ways to set the expiration on a per-key basis. For performing basic string sets, you can either use the SETEX command or provide some additional arguments to your beloved SET command. For all other types of data, you will want to create the key in some way and then follow it with an EXPIRE command against the key. If you want to expire a key at an exact time, you can use the EXPIREAT command and provide it with a specific Unix timestamp integer. Listing 5-40 shows each of these.

Listing 5-40. Methods for Setting Per-Key Expiration

```
SETEX sample 120 "my text"

SET sample "my text" EX 120

MULTI
SET sample "my text"
EXPIRE sample 120
EXEC

EXPIREAT key unix_timestamp
```

Unfortunately, it is not possible to expire entries within a key. For example, you cannot expire an entry inside of a hash or remove an entry from a set.

When setting expiration of data, it is important to pick a good expiration time. These expiration times should be set on a per-entity-type basis. For example, if you cache information about an animal in a zoo that contains the last time the animal was fed, you may want to set the expiration to be an hour. On the other hand, if you cache information about the animal occupancy of a cage, perhaps you set the expiration to a few hours. Of course, this all depends on the consequences of having expired data. Would you accidentally feed the animal twice if the data is 59 minutes outdated? Might you put a sheep in the wolf's cage? Consider worst-case scenarios when choosing expiration times.

Cache Naming Considerations

Naming cache entries can be difficult. A key needs to be as short as possible to accurately describe the data being cached; you need to make sure two separate piece of data could never get the same name. In this section, you'll look at some criteria for generating cache key names.

First, if you are sharing a Redis instance with any other service (shame on you!), you need to namespace your keys with a name representing your service as well as the version of your service (specifically in regard to cache requirements changing). So if you do need a namespace and your service is `animals` and this is the fifth time you've changed your cache strategy, you could prefix all key names with the example in Listing 5-41.

Listing 5-41. Redis Cache Key: Namespace

```
animals-v5-
```

Next you need to describe the type of entity being stored. This entity type may map directly to another microservice in your organization. You also need to include a version for the entity type; if the other service versions their endpoints, you can use that. If they do not version data and even if they promise to never change the data format, don't trust them and instead go with a version of zero. The reason you want to version this data is so that when the upstream service does change its format and you start consuming a new endpoint, you aren't accidentally reading old data left in your cache after you redeploy a service expecting the new data.

As an example, if you consume data from the `animal-type` service, getting data from `/v2/animaltypes`, you may append the string in Listing 5-42 to your key name.

Listing 5-42. Redis Cache Key: Entity Type and Version

```
animaltypes-v2
```

Now things start to get a little trickier. What if the Animal Types service has support for multiple languages? You don't want your German friends to read Monkey or English speakers to read Affe. You now need to add a language identifier to the key name. Really, though, any sort of information that you may pass to the third-party service that can affect the result needs to be added to the key. Listing 5-43 contains your language example.

Listing 5-43. Redis Cache Key: Other Data

```
lang-en_US
```

Finally, once you have enough data to accurately name your key, you need to append an identifier of the individual record to the end of the key. If your service consumes entities from another service and there are potentially a large number of entries, each with their own access patterns, you want to store them as individual records. It may be tempting to shove everything into a single hash, but you then lose out on per-key expiry.

Use a different character than what you've been using before to differentiate the entity collection from the primary key of the entity. I like using a colon myself. If you generate a full key name based on the criteria so far, your complete key may look like the one in Listing 5-44.

Listing 5-44. Redis Cache Key: Entire Key

```
animals-v5-animaltypes-v2-lang-en_US:123
```

Pro tip: When storing language identifiers in key names, if you're using an `Accept-Language` header provided by an end user, don't use the entire thing in the cache key! Those strings are long and dynamic; go as far as to consider them unique per browser. Instead, look at the header, and determine the actual language of the entity to be returned and use that in the key name.

Some things can be tricky to cache. Take into consideration a request made to a service that locates entries around a particular latitude and longitude provided by the user. It may be tempting to insert the latitude and longitude into the key name and cache the results. Unfortunately, what are the odds of two users requesting nearby entries from the same latitude and longitude? This would be fairly low and wouldn't make a good fit for caching. You could consider caching as a low-resolution geohash, but this becomes a tedious battle between CPU and memory.

Another important consideration is user privacy. If, for example, service A requests data from service B and the data is granular based on the user ID, you would need to include the user ID in the key name. There may be other situations where the data changes if a user is an admin or not, but not based on specific user ID, so the key name could contain an admin flag.

Anytime you request data from the cache and you find it, that is called a *cache hit*, and the converse is called a *cache miss*. Whenever you add anything to a cache, consider the ratio of hits and misses. If you're storing a large object and the item is touched infrequently, it might not be worthy of caching. Small data, perhaps which takes 20ms to generate or 10ms to load from cache, if requested frequently enough, may be worthy of inserting into a cache.

Debugging improperly cached data or key collisions can be painful. As an example, imagine you're building service A, which will consume data from service B. Service A downloads data from B and then stores it in the cache. Unfortunately, there's an error in your code, and you mutate the data from service B before adding it to the cache. Now imagine your acceptance tests run, the service grabs the correct data and tests logic that passes, and then the data is corrupted and stored. A subsequent test run would reveal the failure, but only *after* the problem really occurred. It's also common to clear a cache at the beginning of a test run so they're deterministic. With this scenario in mind, do yourself a favor and always make multiple calls for any code related to caching.

Pub/Sub with PUBLISH/SUBSCRIBE

Adding to the long list of features supported by Redis is the notion of Pub/Sub. This is a message-passing pattern wherein clients can subscribe to a "channel" of information, and others can publish to that channel.

This pattern is a little different from other message-passing patterns, such as a job queue. Something to consider is that if no clients are subscribing to a channel when a publish occurs, nobody will get the message (Redis doesn't store the message in a queue). If many clients listen on the same channel, they will all receive the same message (clients do not receive messages round-robin). There is also no ability to acknowledge that a message has been received and acted upon.

When a client decides to subscribe for changes, the client is unable to perform other actions using the same connection to Redis. This is easily remedied by opening multiple connections. You can use the SUBSCRIBE channel [channel2] command to subscribe. There's even a PSUBSCRIBE pattern [pattern2] command for joining multiple channels based on pattern matching (e.g., users.* will match any channel beginning with users).

Run the command in Listing 5-45 within a Redis CLI client to subscribe to two channels, photos and users. This will represent a client subscribing to updates about photo and user resources.

Listing 5-45. Subscribe to Two Channels

```
redis:6379> SUBSCRIBE photos users
1) "subscribe"
2) "photos"
3) (integer)  1
1) "subscribe"
2) "users"
3) (integer)  2
```

Then create a new Redis CLI client in another terminal to represent a provider that emits information about resources. You're going to simulate three events (one for creating a new user, one for deleting a user, and one for sending an e-mail) by running the commands in Listing 5-46.

Listing 5-46. Publish to Different Channels

```
redis:6379> PUBLISH photos '{"action": "new", "id": "1234"}'
(integer) 1

redis:6379> PUBLISH users '{"action": "del", "id": "5678"}'
(integer) 1

redis:6379> PUBLISH emails '{"action": "send", "user_id": "7890"}'
(integer) 0
```

As these commands are being published from your publisher, you should see the two events in Listing 5-47 in your subscriber.

Listing 5-47. Received Messages

```
1) "message"
2) "photos"
3) "{\"action\": \"new\", \"id\": \"1234\"}"

1) "message"
2) "users"
3) "{\"action\": \"del\", \"id\": \"5678\"}"
```

In this case, you see that you receive an event in the photos channel where a photo with ID 1234 was created and the user with ID 5678 was removed. Also, notice that the event on the emails channel was never received. This is to be expected as you were not subscribed to updates from that channel. You may have noticed the return values when the publisher ran the PUBLISH commands; those return values represent the number of clients that should have received the messages.

In these examples, you're sending a small amount of data, just the ID and name of actions happening to resources. You could use this information to do something such as delete an entry from a cache. However, if you were sending an object representing a complete resource, you could go a step further and replace an entry in a cache.

As a more advanced example, imagine you want to build a real-time messaging application. A client can send a message to one of several different service instances (e.g., the requests routed round-robin via HAproxy). Clients make a WebSockets connection to a random service instance. Client 1 (on instance 11) wants to communicate with client 2 (on instance 12). Since instance 12 knows it has client 2 connected, it can use SUBSCRIBE to subscribe to a channel named client-2. When instance 11 receives a message intended for client 2, it will broadcast on that same client-2 channel while also writing the message to an inbox database. If client 2 is connected, the message will be pushed immediately. If the client is offline, the client will see the message the next time they log in and the inbox database is read.

When to Use Redis

Redis is useful in a many different scenarios, such as when the need to access data quickly is important but you don't necessarily need the ability to perform advanced querying, when your data set happens to fit nicely into the existing Redis data structures, when you already have Redis installed in your organization for some other purpose, and when your data set fits into memory.

When Not to Use Redis

If you need the ability to retrieve data based on complex criteria or if the relationships between entities are important, then you may be better off using a SQL database. If you need to alter deeply nested objects represented as JSON, then you would be better off with a tool like CouchDB.

Further Reading: Memcached

Memcached is a fairly popular and older tool for performing in-memory caching of data. It can be used to perform many of the same string operations that Redis supports, has per-key expiry, and even has global LRU settings. The tool has permeated many larger, established organizations and has libraries available for many platforms.

However, Memcached offers a mere subset of the functionality supported by Redis. It does not support the more advanced data structures that Redis has to offer or the ability to run advanced Lua scripting or be used as a Pub/Sub service. There is no noticeable performance difference between the two.

If your organization already uses Memcached and does not want to deal with the additional operational overhead of another in-memory cache and you do not need the advanced features of Redis, then consider using Memcached. Otherwise, Redis should be your first choice.

Document Search with Elasticsearch

Elasticsearch (ES) [56] is a database that is specifically designed to be used for searching for data based on "loose" criteria. Search queries are defined using JSON and can have fairly complex criteria specified. If you've ever wanted to search for records using "fuzzy searching" where the user may be entering multiple words, words that contain typos, and words that may appear in a different order in different sections of a document, then ES may be the tool for you.

Under the hood ES is a document storage database storing objects that can be represented as JSON. That said, you may not want to use ES as a primary data store, instead opting to only store data required for performing search queries. If taking this approach, you can then take the document IDs returned from a search and then retrieve them from another database engine.

When determining what data to keep in ES, keep in mind that since you're working with a copy of data, it might make sense to combine data from different types of resources into a single document. Consider the situation where an organization has a collection of products and a collection of product reviews. A user may want to find text that *should* exist in the product's description but may exist in only a few of the product reviews (e.g., this product contains gluten).

Just like the rest of the database tools you've examined, you can launch Elasticsearch locally with ease using Docker. Run the commands in Listing 5-48 to do so.

Listing 5-48. Running Elasticsearch with Docker

```
$ mkdir -p ~/data/elasticsearch
$ docker run \
    --name my-elasticsearch \
    -p 9200:9200 \
    -p 9300:9300 \
    -v ~/data/elasticsearch:/usr/share/elasticsearch/data \
    -d elasticsearch
```

ES has an HTTP API that you can use to perform any operation you need. This API is rather comprehensive and offers many facilities to do things such as check the health of a cluster of ES nodes. You'll skip most of this, though, and instead perform some simpler actions, specifically creating an index (Listing 5-49), inserting some records, and then searching these records. At this point, you can open your browser to http://localhost:9200 to confirm the ES API is running.

Let's go ahead and create some records that you would like to search. Specifically, you'll be describing the different cages available in a zoo. You'll keep track of the name of the cage as well as a description of the animals inside. You'll also keep track of the geolocation of the cage.

Listing 5-49. Creating an Elasticsearch Index via HTTP

```
$ curl -X PUT -H "Content-Type: application/json" -d '{
  "mappings": {
    "cages": {
      "properties": {
        "location": { "type": "geo_point" },
        "name": { "type": "text" },
        "description": { "type": "text" }
      }
    }
  }
}' "http://localhost:9200/zoo"
```

You can create a few records easily enough by performing the POST requests in Listing 5-50.

Listing 5-50. Inserting Records into Elasticsearch via HTTP

```
$ curl -X PUT -H "Content-Type: application/json" -d '{
    "id": 1, "name": "Penguin Cage I",
    "description": "Contains Emperor Penguins",
    "location": {
      "lat": 37.781358, "lon": -122.4071697
    }
  }'  "http://localhost:9200/zoo/cages/1"
$ curl -X PUT -H "Content-Type: application/json" -d '{
    "id": 2, "name": "Penguin Cage II",
    "description": "Contains Gentoo Penguins and Tux",
    "location": {
      "lat": 37.782418, "lon": -122.4060427
    }
  }'  "http://localhost:9200/zoo/cages/2"
$ curl -X PUT -H "Content-Type: application/json" -d '{
    "id": 3, "name": "Feline Den",
    "description": "Contains Lions and Cheetahs",
    "location": {
      "lat": 37.783215, "lon": -122.4049587
    }
  }'  "http://localhost:9200/zoo/cages/3"
```

By default you can perform simple searches of this data. This can be done by making a GET request to the service and appending a _search parameter to the URL, as shown in Listing 5-51. You get a bunch of information about the returned data, but you specifically care about the hits data.

Listing 5-51. Performing a Simple Elasticsearch Search

```
$ curl -X GET \
"http://localhost:9200/zoo/cages/_search?q=penguins" \
| jq ".hits.hits"
```

This will return all documents that have a text property containing the search term, *penguins,* as shown in Listing 5-52. You also get some meta-information about each hit, with the most notable piece of information being the score. This is a numeric property used for sorting matched documents.

Listing 5-52. Results from Your Simple Search

```
[{
  "_index": "zoo",    "_type": "cages",
  "_id": "1",          "_score": 0.28582606,
  "_source": {
    "id": 1,          "name": "Penguin Cage I",
    "description": "Contains Emperor Penguins",
```

```
      "location":  {
        "lat": 37.781358, "lon": -122.4071697
      }
    }
  }, {
    "_index": "zoo",    "_type": "cages",
    "_id": "2",          "_score": 0.27233246,
    "_source": {
      "id": 2,              "name": "Penguin Cage II",
      "description": "Contains Gentoo Penguins and Tux",
      "location":    {
        "lat": 37.782418, "lon": -122.4060427
      }
    }
  }
}]
```

But this isn't too interesting yet. Let's perform a more complex search where you take the location of cages into consideration.

The query in Listing 5-53 looks a little daunting, but let's look at it piece by piece. There are two main items. The first is the query, which describes the requirements of the data you're retrieving. Afterward is the sort that describes the order in which the results come back. You are creating a Boolean query, which means a document either will or will not match. You are filtering results so that you only get ones within 200 meters of the specified geolocation. You also want records that contain the word *penguins* in their description.

In the sort section you specify that you are sorting based on the distance of the document from the specified location (which is the same as the distance filter you used before). The results are sorted based on ascending distance values so that closer locations come first. You also specify a unit in meters so that in the results you'll be given the distance in meters.

Listing 5-53. Performing a Complex Elasticsearch Search

```
$ curl -X GET "http://localhost:9200/zoo/cages/_search" -d '
{
  "query": {
    "bool": {
      "filter": {
        "geo_distance": {
          "distance": "200m",
          "location": {
            "lat": 37.782842, "lon": -122.4043257
          }
        }
      },
      "must": { "term": { "description": "penguins" } }
    }
```

```
  },
  "sort":  {
    "_geo_distance": {
      "location": { "lat": 37.782842, "lon": -122.4043257 },
      "order": "asc", "unit": "m"
    }
  }
}
' | jq ".hits.hits"
```

Listing 5-54 has the relevant section of the results document. Notice that you get only a single result, which is one of the penguin cages. If you were to modify the request so that the 200 meters limit were then 300 meters, you would receive the second penguin cage as well. The first entry in the sort attribute is the distance in meters.

Listing 5-54. Results from Your Complex Search

```
[{
    "_index": "zoo",  "_type": "cages",
    "_id": "2",        "_score": null,
    "_source": {
      "id": 2,          "name": "Penguin Cage II",
      "description": "Contains Gentoo Penguins and Tux",
      "location": {
      "lat": 37.782418, "lon": -122.4060427
    }
  },
  "sort": [ 158.08883476272732 ]
}]
```

The ability to index and query data in Elasticsearch is much more powerful than the examples you've seen today. It's possible to do things such as fuzzy searches, allowing for typos or plurality changes, scoring results based on multiple criteria such as distance and multiple word occurrences with different weights for each criteria. ES can automatically determine which words are common (e.g., *the* or *and*) and decrease their priority with searching. You can generate descriptions like in a search engine where fragments of sentences around discovered words are returned.

Populating Elasticsearch

Earlier it was mentioned that many organizations choose to use Elasticsearch simply for performing searches, while using another database for being the primary source of truth. In these situations, it's important to keep ES up-to-date with data from the primary data store. If data is outdated, then your searches will provide users with erroneous information. Let's examine a few ways to keep this data correct.

A naive approach is to perform periodical crawls of the entire set of data you want to search. These searches could be performed every night when a product isn't used as frequently. This is the easiest approach to implement but has some major, obvious drawbacks. One is that data will be outdated between 0 and 24 hours. Another is that you may have a lot of perfectly good, nonoutdated data getting thrown away after each crawl. And of course, moving all of this data is taxing, both in CPU usage and in network traffic, which is why you would choose to crawl nightly.

Another approach is to get a list of records changed since the time of the last crawl. When data is stored in a database, you can keep track of the last modification time of the data and query based on it. This allows you to perform periodical crawls more frequently, retrieving only stale entries, and not overwhelming the system. You still have similar issues with the last approach; if you crawl every four hours, then data will be between zero and four hours old. If you crawl every five minutes, you might find that nothing has changed or so much has changed that you can't finish within five minutes.

A more complex approach is that when writes occur in the source-of-truth services, they then make a request to a search service interfacing with ES and update the searchable data in real time. Unfortunately, this adds complexity for the maintainers of each service. You've also shifted the responsibility of maintaining search data from the search team to the product team and introduced some tight coupling.

A more proactive approach for keeping your data updated without introducing tight coupling would be to listen for data changes using a message bus, such as the Pub/Sub feature offered by Redis. When your product service writes a change to a database, it could also publish a change event for that product. The search service could subscribe to changes for both products and product reviews, updating ES with the new data when changes have occurred.

CHAPTER 6

Consumers

You need to keep many things in mind when dealing with consumers, particularly in regard to keeping track of them. You need to know who a consumer is, which can be done either by looking at a user agent or by performing authentication. You need to version your endpoint and keep track of which version consumers use so you can later deprecate a version. And when consumers of a public application programming interface (API) start hogging resources, you need to cut them off.

User Agents

Whenever a request enters your service, it should contain a user agent, a string used to represent the client making the request. By default these are usually generic; for example, a common Python library sends the header `python-requests/2.2.1`, which does little to tell you *who* sent the request.

What your organization needs to do is enforce some rules around user agent naming. Require that those who consume your service send a well-formed and meaningful user agent. Of course, any outbound requests generated from your service should follow these same guidelines.

You pass around (and require) user agents so that you can include them in your logs and communicate with those making requests.

Let's pretend you live in a world without user agents. Imagine your application is running just fine. It's Wednesday afternoon, and you've just returned from lunch. You pull up your log monitoring software, and you see a large spike in errors originating at 1 p.m. This is affecting 25 percent of all inbound requests! How do you find the source of these errors?

At this point, you can examine the logs, looking at the parameters and endpoints the requests are coming from, and try to guess the service. You may start sending messages or asking nearby members of other teams. Or perhaps you start looking through deployment logs and figure out who deployed the erroneous code at 1 p.m. It's not a fun way to spend Wednesday afternoon indeed.

On the other hand, if you enforce proper user agent conventions, you could look at the logs, see that they always come from the same service, and contact the owners to notify them of the errors.

© Thomas Hunter II 2017
T. Hunter II, *Advanced Microservices*, DOI 10.1007/978-1-4842-2887-6_6

> **Collaboration Tip**: Always assume the other teams and services in your organization do not adhere to the same disciplined monitoring practices that your team does. Proactively alert other teams when their project becomes faulty so that they can triage and so the organization can return to a healthy state as soon as possible.

User agents (RFC 2616 14.43 [10]) are pretty simple to deal with. First come up with a name for your application using lowercase letters, numbers, and hyphens. An example of this could be photos if your service deals with all the photo storage requirements of the organization, as shown in Listing 6-1 as a complete header. This is enough information to properly identify your application to other services.

Listing 6-1. Example User Agent Header

```
User-Agent: photos
```

However, you can be a little more specific. What do you do if a deployment partially failed? Perhaps you have two versions of your service running in parallel. Or one day another team is performing some archeology of old logs and notices errors. Nobody will remember what version was running on that date without tedious cross-references of commits and deploy logs.

To get around this shortcoming, you can include information about the version of the service in the request. The most common method for doing this is to separate the name of the user agent with a slash and then provide the version number. Most service maintainers don't seem to version their service, so a hash representing the last commit is equally useful for performing root-cause analysis. You can see these two methods in Listing 6-2.

Listing 6-2. Example User Agent Header with Version

```
User-Agent: photos/1.1.2
User-Agent: photos/cd5906b7685d
```

API Versioning

No matter what you are building and how much planning you do beforehand, your core application will change, your company will pivot, your data relationships will alter, and attributes will be changed and removed from resources. This is just how software development works and is especially true if your project is under active development and used by many people.

Remember that an API is a published contract between a server and a consumer. If you make changes to the API and these changes break backward compatibility, you will break deployed applications, and developers will resent you for it. Do it enough, and they may migrate to somebody else's service. To ensure your application continually evolves *and* you keep developers happy, you need to occasionally introduce new versions of the API while still allowing old versions to function.

Facebook is notorious for making backward-breaking changes to its API. I've had my fair share of Facebook applications get rendered useless after a breaking change was made. Even while researching their Graph API, I could not find any mention of a scheme for performing versioning. Don't be like Facebook.

▓ **Note**   If you are simply *adding* new features to your API, such as new attributes to a resource (assuming they are not required to be set), or if you are *adding* new endpoints, you do not need to increment your API version number because these changes do not break backward compatibility. You will of course want to update your API documentation.

Over time you can deprecate old versions of the API. Deprecating a feature doesn't mean to shut if off or diminish quality but to alert developers that the older version will be removed on a specific date and that they should upgrade to a newer version.

You'll now examine some different methods for performing API versioning. Make sure you support only one method per service (e.g., don't combine version URL segments with version headers).

> **Collaboration Tip**: Try to adopt a single method for performing API versioning across your entire organization. This will make life much easier for services that consume many other services.

Versioning via URL Segment

The method that is the easiest for most consumers to handle is to add a URL segment between the root location of the API and specific endpoints, as shown in Listing 6-3. Changing the URL is the easiest thing a developer can do.

The most common argument against this approach is that /v1/users and /v2/users supposedly represent the same data, and using redundant URLs for the same data violates good HTTP design principles. However, the two URLs likely *do not* represent the same data because one could be abstracting data completely differently than the other. There's also no guarantee endpoints will be named the same between versions because their concepts may differ.

Consider an API that has the concept of a separate user and a business. However, the product one day merges the two concepts into a single resource called an *organization*. In this case, the resources are namespaced after the version endpoint (/v1/users, /v1/businesses, /v2/organizations) in a way that would feel awkward with headers.

Listing 6-3. Version in URL

```
https://api.example.org/v1/*
```

It is customary to use the letter **v** followed by an integer when versioning this way. Because of the nature of APIs, changing versions often is discouraged, so point releases usually aren't needed.

LinkedIn and Google+ use a **v** and an integer (e.g., /v3/). Dropbox just uses an integer (e.g., /1/). Twitter uses a **v** and a decimal (e.g., /v1.1/). Netflix uses a ?v= and a decimal URL parameter (not an endpoint URL segment but still part of the URL).

Versioning via the Accept Header

Another common approach is to use a custom `Accept` header where the consumer specifies the type of content expected along with the version of the API. This method may be the *purest* as far as RESTful API design is concerned. See it in action in Listing 6-4.

The `Accept` header offers a way to specify generic and less generic content types as well as specifying fallbacks. In Listing 6-4 you are requesting a more specific version of JSON, conceptually version 1 of the API JSON.

Listing 6-4. Version in Accept Header

```
Accept: application/json+v1
```

GitHub uses an `Accept` header formatted as `application/vnd.github.v3+json` to interact with a specific version of its API. If the `Accept` header is omitted, the consumer interacts with the *beta* (latest) version.

Versioning via a Custom Header

Another method is to use a custom header like the one shown in Listing 6-5. This is quite similar to the previous method. Consumers would still use the normal `Accept` header they've been using and add this new one.

Listing 6-5. Version in a Version Header

```
X-Api-Version: 1
```

The Joyent CloudAPI and Copy.com APIs use this header.

API Deprecation

When your service does decide to deprecate an endpoint, stop using a particular version of endpoints, or even shut down entirely, you should reach out and contact the consumers of your service and let them know.

Assuming this is an internal service, it shouldn't be hard to track down the teams that own the consumers and let them know. Of course, you'll want to send plenty of notice, perhaps a month if an alternative endpoint exists and is comparable to the old one. However, if this is going to be a major change with a difficult migration path, you'll want to send feedback much further in advance.

> **Collaboration Tip**: If it's in *your* best interest to get users of an old endpoint to use a new version (say it crashes your server less or uses fewer resources), then it may be your duty to proactively contribute a change to the consuming service. Send them a pull request or e-mail them a detailed migration path. If a different team can't dedicate the time to upgrade, then your boss may not approve the deprecation.

If this service is consumed by third parties, you'll want to update your documentation, send a message to a mailing list, and so on. You'll also want to give much longer notice. If you have hundreds of different consumers, it only stands to reason that a few of them are on vacation.

Authentication and Authorization

Authentication is the process of verifying who a user is such as by providing a username and password. Authorization is determining which resources that user has access to and what actions that user is able to perform. Collectively you can refer to these two terms as *auth.*

There are two common paradigms in which your API may authenticate consumers. Using the two-legged paradigm, there are two parties involved: a consumer and your provider. In the two-legged paradigm there are three parties involved, namely, a consumer, your provider, and a user who has (or will have) an account with both services.

In theory, your API could use both methods of authentication for different areas. Also, there may be some sections of the API that can be accessed anonymously and can entirely bypass the authentication process.

> **Collaboration Tip**: Auth is mostly useful for services that are exposed to the outside world or services that are in a multitenant environment. Think twice before locking down an internal API and requiring teammates to register to use it because this may add unnecessary overhead. However, in environments where security is the utmost concern such as in financial organizations, it may make sense to require auth on internal services.

Two-Legged Authentication (2LA)

As you can see in Figure 6-1, the concept of two-legged authentication is quite simple. Essentially the consumer needs a way to authenticate themselves with a service provider. Because of the stateless nature of HTTP, this authentication needs to be present with every request.

Figure 6-1. *Two-legged authentication*

Modern web sites make use of sessions for handling this state using a session identifier that is passed along with every request via a cookie. With an API you wouldn't require the use of a cookie (they're typically difficult to work with programmatically), but the method you will use is similar.

> The introduction of site-wide state information in the form of HTTP cookies is an example of an inappropriate extension to the protocol. Cookie interaction fails to match REST's application state model, often resulting in confusion for the typical browser application. [57, Page 145]

HTTP defines a header called Authorization for passing around this sort of information. While there are many different approaches for implementing API authorization, many of them leverage this header in some manner.

Basic HTTP Authentication

The *classical* method of performing authentication is called Basic HTTP Auth [9] where a user agent (meaning a web browser or consumer) first makes a GET request to a protected resource (see Listing 6-6). The server responds with the 401 Unauthorized header (shown in Listing 6-7), and the user agent displays a dialog prompting the user for a username and password (as shown in Figure 6-2).

Listing 6-6. Initial Request

```
GET /protected HTTP/1.1
Host: www.example.org
Accept: text/html
```

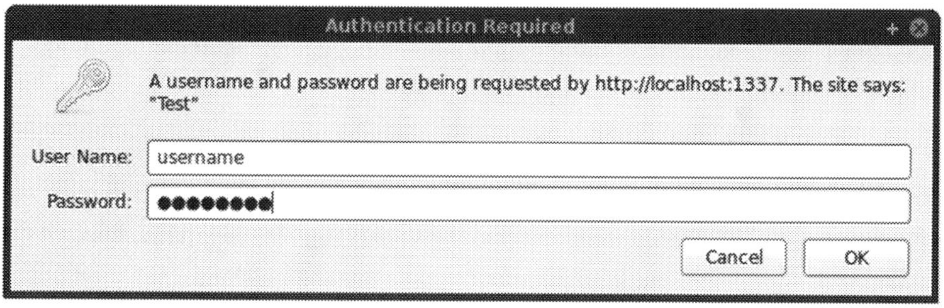

Figure 6-2. *Basic HTTP authentication dialog in Firefox*

Listing 6-7. Unauthorized Response

```
HTTP/1.1 401 Unauthorized
Date: Thu, 9 Jan 2014 23:35:00 GMT
WWW-Authenticate: Basic realm="Example"
```

At this point the user either clicks Cancel and is taken to an error screen and chooses to go somewhere else or they enter correct credentials and click Authorize. Entering the wrong credentials typically results in the server sending back the same Unauthorized status.

The credentials supplied by the user are transmitted as follows: the username (which cannot contain :) is concatenated with : and then concatenated with the password. This text is then Base64 encoded and sent in the authorization header, shown in Listing 6-8. As you can probably guess, this is extremely insecure if done over unencrypted HTTP.

Listing 6-8. Authorized Request

```
GET /protected HTTP/1.1
Host: www.example.org
Accept: text/html
Authorization: Basic QWxhZGRpbjpvcGVuIHNlc2FtZQ==
```

Finally, the server provides the user agent with the protected content that the user has requested. This same authorization header is sent with every subsequent request.

Implementing HTTP Basic Authorization in your API is just as easy except that instead of having a browser on the other end, it would be a consumer of your API. The initial unauthorized request doesn't need to be performed because the consumer would know ahead of time that it needs to first be authorized. If the consumer does provide incorrect credentials, the server would still reply with a 401 Unauthorized status.

Alternatives to Basic Auth

You could invent your own method of auth where you supply the consumer with a single randomly generated and impossible-to-guess token that the consumer simply provides in the Authorization header (this concept is often referred to as an *auth token*).

Third parties may want the ability to revoke auth tokens and to generate multiple ones for their application. Make sure you provide an administration interface so developers can provision and revoke these tokens themselves.

Three-Legged Authentication (3LA)

As you can see in Figure 6-3, 3LA is a bit more complex. Instead of passing messages between two parties (one channel), messages need to be communicated between three parties (three channels). A user likely trusts your application with their username and password; however, they don't trust a third-party consumer. The user would also like the ability to revoke the third party's access to the data without the need to change the username and password.

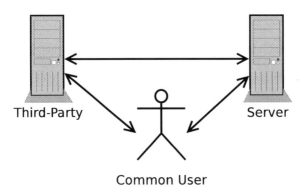

Figure 6-3. *Three-legged authentication*

The complexities of 3LA are far too intricate to exemplify in this book, so you'll want to read more information from a different source. At a high level, they provide a method for a consumer to sign requests and to validate they are who they say they are. 3LA also provides a method for users to grant privileges so consumers can access specific data. Users can revoke permissions from consumers at any point. Of course, the server can also revoke a consumer's privileges.

OAuth 2.0 [58] is the de facto standard for performing 3LA in modern HTTP APIs. With each request the server can be sure it knows which consumer is making a request and which user they are making requests on behalf of, and the server provides a standardized method for expiring access or allowing users to revoke access from a consumer, all without the need for a third-party consumer to know the user's login credentials.

There is also the older OAuth 1.0a [59] standard, which solves mostly the same problems. This standard works by requiring a hash of OAuth attributes sent over the wire, which includes concepts such as a timestamp and a nonce. These are common in cryptographic systems for providing security such as preventing replay attacks and are mostly made irrelevant by sending data over HTTPS. Whichever method you ultimately choose, ensure it is trustworthy and well-documented and has many different libraries available for the languages and platforms that your consumers will likely be using.

OAuth 1.0a, while it is technically the most secure of the options, can be quite difficult to implement. While maintaining an OAuth 1.0a provider for Copy.com, I was surprised by the number of developers who had to implement their own library since one didn't already exist for their language! After spending many days debugging cryptic "invalid signature" errors, I really must suggest choosing OAuth 2.0.

Real-World Usage

Choosing which authentication mechanism to use for your service may be made easier by looking at what other products use and their reasoning for choosing each method.

- *Twitter*: OAuth 1.0a, xAuth (proprietary), OAuth 2.0

  - OAuth 1.0a is kept around to support legacy consumers.

  - xAuth was created to bring some OAuth 2.0 features to OAuth 1.0a (e.g., desktop login).

- *GitHub*: OAuth 2.0, Basic Auth

  - Basic Auth will leak user credentials to third parties.

  - Basic Auth was likely chosen for developers testing their own apps.

  - GitHub users *are* developers after all.

- *Mailgun*: Basic Auth

  - Mailgun is purely 2LA, so Basic Auth is a fine choice.

  - Using Basic Auth makes it easier for novice developers to test the API.

- *Facebook Graph*: OAuth 2.0

  - The user base is Facebook's greatest asset and is definitely a 3LA service.

  - Facebook is a big target for hackers.

- *Dropbox*: OAuth 1.0a, OAuth 2.0

  - OAuth 1.0a is for supporting legacy consumers.

  - OAuth 2.0 is the preferred method for authenticating with Dropbox.

Consumer Permissions

Permissions are a way of specifying which consumers have access to what data and more specifically how they are allowed to manipulate this data.

When dealing with 2LA, the process for deciding permissions is likely to be handled simply. For example, if your service is owned by Widgets Inc. and this company trusts Gadgets Co. with certain features of the API, Widgets Inc. will probably manually assign Gadgets Co. with more liberal permissions. However, the company Hackers LLC, which is otherwise unknown to Widgets Inc., will get the default restrictive permissions. Or perhaps additional permissions can be earned by paying a fee or mailing in a photo ID.

Regarding 3LA, the consumer needs to have the ability to specify which resources belonging to the user the consumer would like to interact with. When the user authorizes the consumer, the user is usually prompted with a GUI to review permissions, perhaps make a decision or two, and either allow or deny access. You've likely seen these permission prompts with services such as Twitter (shown in Figure 6-4), Facebook, LinkedIn, and so on.

Some services will allow a user to disable permissions (older versions of Facebook allowed this), whereas other services will require the permissions to be accepted or denied outright. You can choose whichever approach you'd like with your service.

Authorize Hackspace to use your account?

This application will be able to:

- Read Tweets from your timeline.
- See who you follow.

Sign In　**Cancel**

This application **will not be able to**:

- Follow new people.
- Update your profile.
- Post Tweets for you.
- Access your direct messages.
- See your Twitter password.

Hackspace
www.hackspace.org
Find local places to get work done.

Figure 6-4. *Twitter OAuth permissions*

Per-Authorization Permissions

The method for specifying permissions will vary depending on the authorization mechanism your API implements. With OAuth 1.0a, a standard didn't exist as part of the spec. The server can accept an additional parameter called scope (or whatever you choose) during the request token generation phase. This parameter could be a JSON object representing the permissions the consumer is requesting. By passing this parameter during the authorization step, a consumer is able to get per-user permissions.

The permissions object in Listing 6-9 could represent a common social media web site. It represents a consumer that wants to get information about a user's profile as well as make changes to the profile, send the user e-mails using the service (although not have access to the e-mail address), retrieve a list of friends, add new friends, and remove existing friends.

Listing 6-9. Example JSON Permissions

```
{
  "profile": [ "read", "write" ],
  "email": [ "send" ],
  "friends": [ "read", "add", "remove" ]
}
```

When the user authenticates the consumer, the user would see a list of each of the permissions the consumer is asking for. Some of them that grant destructive or powerful capabilities such as adding and removing friends or changing the user's profile should be emphasized.

Listing 6-10 shows an example taken from Coinbase [60]. Coinbase adheres to the OAuth 2.0 spec for sending permissions by using a simple list of keywords representing permissions separated by spaces (which are encoded as + symbols). This request would allow the consumer to buy, sell, send, and request Bitcoins on behalf of the authenticated user.

Listing 6-10. Example Coinbase Permissions

```
https://coinbase.com/oauth/authorize?response_type=code
    &client_id=YOUR_CLIENT_ID&redirect_uri=YOUR_CALLBACK_URL
    &scope=buy+sell+send+request
```

Default Consumer Permissions

When a consumer registers an application with your server, assuming permissions will need to be the same for every user of their application, the consumer can specify the permissions all at once. This would probably be done from a UI such as providing a list of check boxes where each check box represents a permission. Figure 6-5 shows an example of per-consumer permissions used by Copy.com.

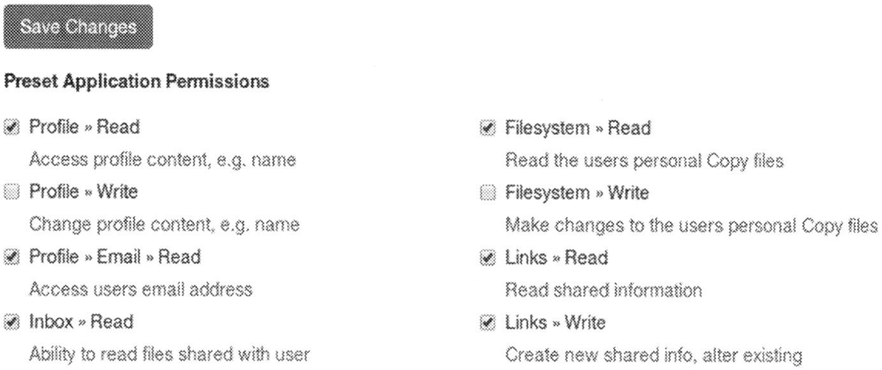

Figure 6-5. *Copy.com default consumer permissions*

Ideally your server could even allow for both of these mechanisms to work in parallel (accepting preset permissions, to be overwritten by optional per-user permissions). This gives developers the greatest amount of control and convenience.

Rate Limiting

Rate limiting is a feature that can be implemented in a service to prevent consumers from diminishing stability by making too many requests. Consumers can be given a limit on the number of requests they make. This limit could be per consumer, per user per consumer, or whatever you decide. If limits are per consumer, then depending on how much your server trusts the consumer, the limits could be higher. Some services even offer a subscription fee for increasing this limit.

Rate limiting should not be enforced if your service is consumed only internally. It should be enforced only at the furthest point downstream where user requests first enter your organization.

If your service makes use of rate limits, be sure information about the limit can be accessed programmatically. Listing 6-11 shows an example of how GitHub conveys rate limit information to third parties with the introduction of X-RateLimit headers. The -Limit header represents the total limit per period of time, -Remaining is how many requests remain to be made during this period of time, and -Reset is a timestamp for when the period resets.

Listing 6-11. Example of Exceeding GitHub's Rate Limit

```
HTTP/1.1 403 Forbidden
Date: Tue, 20 Aug 2013 14:50:41 GMT
Status: 403 Forbidden
X-RateLimit-Limit: 60
X-RateLimit-Remaining: 0
X-RateLimit-Reset: 1377013266

{
    "message": "API rate limit exceeded. \
        See http://developer.github.com/v3/ \
        #rate-limiting for details."
}
```

CHAPTER 7

Monitoring

In this chapter, I will cover the topic of monitoring the livelihood of your service. There are three types of tools I will use to do so. Logging will allow you to view granular information about each request your service handles. Analytics will allow you to view overall statistics-aggregating information about all requests. Finally, alerting allows you to be paged when your service is no longer healthy.

Logging

Logging is a vital part of keeping your microservice alive and healthy. Logs contain valuable information such as stack traces and information about where data is coming from and can help you reassemble the crime scene of a server crash.

SSHing into a machine and looking at STDOUT may work if you have a single instance running, but in the world of highly available and redundant microservices, you need to aggregate all those logs to a common place. You also need the ability to query those logs based on different criteria. For example, if a single instance is bad, you might want to look at the process ID (PID), hostname, and port.

Another interesting part about logging is that you'll even need to look at logs from services owned by different teams within the organization. Finding out which logs from another service correlate with a failed request from your service is another sleuthing skill this chapter will teach you.

ELK: Elasticsearch, Logstash, Kibana

If you'd like to run an in-house stack for aggregating, querying, and displaying logs, consider the Elasticsearch, Logstash, Kibana (ELK) stack (see Figure 7-1), all three of which are open source tools maintained by Elastic.

Kibana [61] is a graphical tool for displaying time-series log data. Logs can be displayed as simple rows of textual data as well as graphs. Data can be queried based on the values of fields. For example, you could query all 5XX errors received within a certain application during last Tuesday. Complex dashboards can be created using Kibana.

© Thomas Hunter II 2017

T. Hunter II, *Advanced Microservices*, DOI 10.1007/978-1-4842-2887-6_7

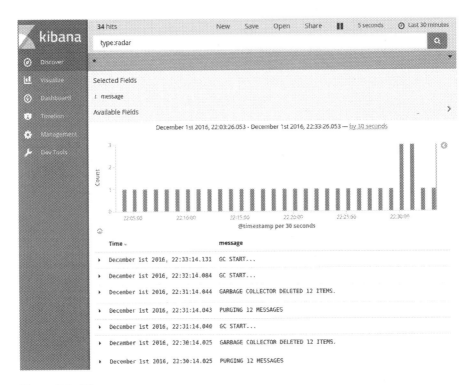

Figure 7-1. *Kibana*

Elasticsearch [56] is a flexible document database engine that specializes in the ability to write interesting queries to get insight into your data. It is frequently used in applications for providing search functionality. It provides a RESTful interface and has many client libraries available. In the scope of the ELK stack, it is used for persisting your logs.

Logstash [62] is a tool for consuming and transforming log data provided in many different formats into a clean and consistent format. It can do things such as listen for JSON being sent via User Datagram Protocol (UDP), read Nginx or Apache log files, and parse syslog logs. It can even provide more powerful transformations requiring outside data such as converting IP addresses into geolocations. There are many open source libraries available in different languages for sending data to Logstash.

Transmitting Logs via Logstash

With Logstash being the tool that ingests logs, let's first configure it so that your application can send logs to it. A common approach is to transmit logs via UDP. This doesn't guarantee logs will be delivered, but it does allow you to send tons of logs without adding too much congestion.

In your Logstash configuration (depending on your distribution, you may be able to create a file such as /etc/logstash/conf.d/20-udp.conf and restart the service), add an entry that looks like Listing 7-1.

Listing 7-1. Configuring Logstash for UDP

```
input {
    udp {
        port => 5959
        host  => "0.0.0.0"
        codec => "json"
    }
}
```

The port 5959 is just something I made up; feel free to use whatever you'd like. The host entry defaults to 0.0.0.0 for all connections, but you can change it to localhost if you'd like to receive only internal requests.

After the configuration has been added, restart the service (this may be as easy as $ sudo service logstash restart), and Logstash should now be listening for properly formed JSON data sent via UDP. You can now start sending messages from your application using whatever libraries are available.

The messages you send need to adhere to a common format. The library you use will require some configuration (such as naming your application) and will provide the basic attributes for you when transmitting a log (such as the current time).

Listing 7-2 shows an example of what a Logstash log might look like.

Listing 7-2. Example Logstash Log Entry

```
{
    "@timestamp": "2017-01-01T13:37:15.185Z",
    "@version": "1",
    "fields": {
        "category": "server",
        "purged": "23",
        "level": "DEBUG"
    },
    "message": "Global Garbage Collection Finished.",
    "type": "radar"
}
```

Most of these fields have been provided by the library I'm using in my application. The message and purged values I've provided on a per-log basis, with the level value being named after the method I'm calling (e.g., logger.debug() in this case). So, the log call in my code may look as simple as Listing 7-3.

Listing 7-3. Example Application Code for Calling Logstash

```
logger.debug("Global Garbage Collection Finished.", {
  "purged": 23
});
```

Collaboration Tip: Standardize your logging structure across the organization. Make sure that every team is sending a well-formed name of their application. Whenever logging HTTP requests, be sure to log the amount of time it took to make the request, the resulting status code, any applicable headers, etc., and make sure the name of the fields are consistent across projects. This will allow you to easily duplicate dashboards and allow for immediate familiarity when moving between projects.

Querying Logs via Kibana

Now that you've been writing some log data, it's time to start querying it. Load up the web interface for Kibana and visit the Discover section so that you can write some ad hoc queries. You can use the Lucene query syntax [63] to write some queries.

The interface is quite easy to use once you get the hang of it. The time range you would like to use can be set using the header. The query bar will allow you to put in all other criteria.

If you'd like to query against anything for any particular string, just type the string in, as in Listing 7-4.

Listing 7-4. Simple Kibana Text Search

```
Garbage Collection
```

Of course, you want to be more specific. If you'd like to query based on the name of your application, you can enter a key/value pair like you see in Listing 7-5.

Listing 7-5. Kibana Key/Value Search

```
type:radar
```

Now you're getting somewhere. If you'd like to combine multiple entries, you can separate them with the AND Boolean operator like in Listing 7-6.

Listing 7-6. Kibana Boolean Operator

```
type:radar AND status:500
```

Querying based on ranges can be more beneficial for things such as reading status codes. To do that, use the range operator, as shown in Listing 7-7.

Listing 7-7. Kibana Querying by Range

```
status:[500 TO 599]
```

For more advanced queries or to learn how to convert your queries into permanent dashboards, you will want to read the official Kibana documentation.

Request UUID Tracking

When an initial HTTP request is made by an end user and it enters your organization's ecosystem of microservices, this request may ultimately generate requests to several services before sending a response back to the user. When this happens, any number of things could happen. One of the services could be slow, thereby making the entire request slow. One of the services could fail, making the entire request fail. One service could leave data in an unexpected state, emitting a warning somewhere, and hunting that warning down could be a real pain.

Luckily, there is a simple solution for keeping track of these requests and connecting them all.

When a request first enters, the system generates a unique identifier for this request. Of course, with the distributed nature of microservices, you can't simply set this value to an ever-incrementing integer. Instead, you want to make use of a UUID, which is a large, randomly generated value having a small chance of collision. A UUID looks like the value in Listing 7-8.

Listing 7-8. Example of a UUID

```
0c8bc16e-deb1-4021-9641-95767e3550b9
```

Once this identifier is generated, pass it along to every underlying service in the form of an HTTP header. You can see an example of how to query this header in Listing 7-9.

> **Collaboration Tip**: What you name the header isn't as important as keeping it consistent throughout all services. There isn't really a "standard" for this, so choose whatever works for your organization.

Listing 7-9. Querying for a Request ID Header

```
X-Request-ID: 0c8bc16e-deb1-4021-9641-95767e3550b9
```

Every service within your organization that creates outbound requests within the context of an inbound request needs to pass this same header along. Any generated logs that correlate to work being performed with the intent of providing data for a request with an ID should log this ID in a standardized manner. (Any asynchronous work not associated with a request won't have a request ID.)

Once you have every system logging in the same manner, you can use your logging interface (e.g., Kibana) to filter related requests. These requests should be provided to the client in some sort of way so that an engineer or QA person can find them and report them to a developer to analyze. By combining these logs from disparate systems, you form a sort of timeline representing the request and are able to easily answer the question, "Why did this request fail?"

Dynamic Log Verbosity

Nearly all logging libraries will allow the developer to set different levels of seriousness with each message being logged. There isn't really a universal standard for log levels, but most libraries seem to implement the following levels: DEBUG, INFO, WARN, ERROR, FATAL. These levels increase in seriousness from left to right.

Any decent logging library will also allow you to set the logging threshold when the application begins. For example, having a threshold set to WARN means that only messages of level WARN or greater will be logged. Anything less will simply be ignored. This is nice because you don't need to write application logic to remove logs from your code when you deploy to production.

These levels are mostly configured based on the environment in which the service is running. On your development machine, you probably want to see as much information as possible. Your application may be configured at the level of INFO to achieve this. However, keeping track of all these messages can start to add up if you're sending them to a logging service. This means in production you might set the threshold to WARN.

A common (and painful) debugging experience is the situation in which the application has caused an error and you actually do want all of those noisy INFO messages on production. Do you temporarily change the threshold and deploy code so that you can reproduce the issue in production, all the while overwhelming your logging server only to roll back the threshold when you're done?

A better approach for these situations is to queue up *all* logs related to a particular group of work, for example, an HTTP request, and only when an error occurs do you transmit the messages. This may be tricky to implement and will require some intelligent logging tools but can be worth it. If you take this approach, you transmit noisy messages only when you absolutely need to do so.

Analytics

Analytics tools will allow you to view a dashboard containing overall service information. These dashboards should make it painfully obvious to someone not on your team if your service is healthy. Being able to tell when an incident began and ended as well as the number of affected users is imperative.

Keep track of the version/endpoints being used by consumers of your API. This can be as simple as incrementing an integer in a database each time a request is made. There are many reasons that keeping track of API analytics is beneficial, such as optimizing the most commonly requested endpoints to reduce server load.

When you do deprecate a version of your API, you can actually contact third-party developers using deprecated features. This is a convenient approach for reminding developers to upgrade before killing off the old version.

Try to keep track of a matrix worth of analytics data, such as which endpoint is used, in which version of the API, and by which consumer (and perhaps even which 3LA user, if applicable). If you get angry users telling you that certain features are broken, then having this information will be helpful for diagnosing problems.

Grafana, Graphite, and StatsD

If you'd like to run an analytics stack in-house (which means installing the required services, configuration, and managing data), then this section is for you.

Grafana [64] is a tool for graphically displaying data tracked over time. There are many ways you can create graphs in Grafana. One graph can display multiple queries at once as different series, with dynamic values in queries generating multiple series per query. Data can be displayed in multiple units such as bytes or percents, linearly or logarithmically, with the ability to choose colors. You can even calculate and display aggregate stats.

Figure 7-2 shows Grafana displaying time-series data.

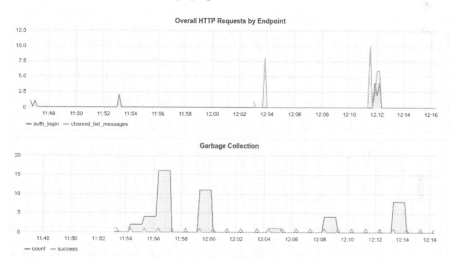

Figure 7-2. *Grafana displaying time-series data*

Graphite [65] is a tool for numeric time-series data. Part of this is a daemon called Carbon, which listens for incoming metrics before writing to a database. Another component is Whisper, which is a database for storing metrics. Finally, you also need Graphite-Web or Graphite-API configured so that Grafana can read the data.

StatsD [66] is a daemon that listens for stats transmitted via TCP or UDP and transmits them to Graphite. The sorts of stats it collects are timing and counting data, which is tracked at certain times.

Transmitting Data via StatsD

Collaboration Tip: Try to standardize the stats hierarchy as an organization and have different teams implement the same standard. Assuming an organization-wide standard is adopted, you can easily create templates in Graphite and reuse them across teams by changing the service name. Consider creating shared libraries that plug into web frameworks or request libraries and abstract the calls away from application developers.

137

StatsD messages are simple to transmit. They can be sent using simple TCP or UDP packets and have a simple format, as shown in Listing 7-10.

Listing 7-10. StatsD Message Syntax

```
<metricname>:<value>|<type>
```

Listing 7-11 shows an example message that will increment a stat used to represent the number of times the photo service crashes.

Listing 7-11. StatsD Increment Photos Crash

```
service.photos.crashes:1|c
```

There are several different metric types for StatsD [67], listed next. You will likely find yourself mostly using counting calls, using a few timing calls, and barely using the rest.

- Counting/sampling is used for keeping track of simple numeric values that increment such as the number of times an endpoint has been requested.

- Timing is used for keeping track of how long something took such as the time to respond to a request or get data from a database.

- Gauges are used for setting arbitrary values that will be persisted until another one is sent. This could be used to represent the number of users logged into a site at once where you set the gauge only when a change occurs.

- Sets are used for counting the number of unique events based on a namespace. By sending user IDs to a set for every request, you know the number of unique users making requests.

If you want to test that StatsD is running properly, you can issue the Listing 7-12 one-liner in your terminal (assuming it is running on the local machine).

Listing 7-12. StatsD Test Command

```
$ echo "foo:1|c" | nc -u -w0 127.0.0.1 8125
```

Data is stored (and later queried) using a hierarchy. The periods in the metric name strings are used for separating levels within this hierarchy. You can sort of think of these as folders. The last segment of the metric name string is used for storing actual values. You can think of these as files.

You're able to query this data using dynamic segments in the metric names (covered more in the "Querying Data via Grafana" section), but there is a caveat to this approach. You'll never want to have files and folders in the same folder. The following is an example of why.

Pretend you have two services that you rely on, alpha and beta. You want to keep track of how much time it takes for each of them to respond. You also want to further break this down and see how much time it takes them to respond on a per-status code basis. Listing 7-13 shows a naive solution for this.

Listing 7-13. Naive Approach to StatsD

```
service.timing.alpha:100|ms
service.timing.beta:200|ms
service.timing.alpha.404:100|ms
```

Unfortunately, you cannot query `service.timing.*` to get a list of all service timing data because your tools will get confused when they encounter the millisecond timings sitting next to the status codes.

The approach in Listing 7-14 meets your requirements.

Listing 7-14. Better Approach to StatsD

```
service.timing.alpha.timing:100|ms
service.timing.beta.timing:200|ms
service.timing.alpha.status.404:100|ms
```

You can then query `service.timing.*.timing` for a list of all services and the speed they take to respond.

The messages shown earlier are what is sent over the wire, but luckily there are a lot of libraries for making StatsD calls.

These libraries are going to abstract most of the work for you. For example, a common prefix to represent your service will probably be set at instantiation, and instead of concatenating colon and pipes and numbers, you'll probably be making different method calls.

Querying Data via Grafana

Using the Grafana web interface, you can write Graphite queries to get information from your data.

Wildcards

As you've seen before, you can make use of asterisks to represent wildcards for a certain segment. Consider the example in Listing 7-15.

Listing 7-15. StatsD Wildcards

```
x.*.z
```

This will grab data such as `x.y1.z`, `x.y2.z`, and so on. However, you sometimes only want to grab a finite number of items where you know the names ahead of time. In those cases, you can use curly braces and commas to specify which items you want to grab, as shown in Listing 7-16.

Listing 7-16. StatsD-Specific Items

```
status.{warning,error}.count
```

This will grab the items `status.warning.count` and `status.error.count`, but unlike its asterisk counterpart will not capture `status.success.count`.

Suffix Attributes and Root Elements

When querying data, even if you add data at a certain point in the hierarchy, you can't actually access the values until you append an additional suffix segment to the path. Even the prefix needs to be changed a little bit.

In this example, my application emits the counter stats shown in Listing 7-17.

Listing 7-17. Emitting Simple Data with StatsD

```
foo:1|c
```

To actually get that data in Grafana, add some prefixes and one of two suffixes, as shown in Listing 7-18.

Listing 7-18. StatsD Prefixes and Suffixes

```
stats.counters.foo.count
stats.counters.foo.rate
```

The prefixes appear to be added at the StatsD level. The type of data is the next segment of the hierarchy (in this case all `counters`). After that comes the path you define in code (a simple `foo` in this case). Finally, you get access to two suffixes, namely, `count` and `rate`. The first value, `count`, is the raw number of items you've added. The second value, `rate`, is the number of items that are being counted per second.

When using timers, there are even more suffixes. Suffixes such as `mean`, `sum`, and `upper_ 95` are some of the suffixes available, with each doing different aggregate math for you.

Graphite Functions

There are many different Graphite functions [68] at your disposal. Queries can contain multiple functions and even functions nested within functions. The Graphite querying language is surprisingly powerful! I'm only going to mention my favorite one to give you a taste, so check out the documentation if you would like to learn more.

When querying with wildcards, the resulting series name of the graph will be the entire matched record. This can get very unwieldly. Luckily, there is a function for renaming the queries based on which wildcards you're matching, as shown in Listing 7-19.

Listing 7-19. Wrapping Your Query with a Graphite Function

```
stats.counters.my-app.http.out.*.200.count
aliasByNode(stats.counters.my-app.http.out.*.200.count, 3, 5)
```

When using the previous queries and assuming you have only two items matched with the asterisk, you'll match the entries shown in Listing 7-20 and Listing 7-21.

Listing 7-20. Series Names from First Query

```
stats.counters.my-app.http.out.service1.200.count
stats.counters.my-app.http.out.service2.200.count
```

Listing 7-21. Series Names from Second Query

```
http.service1
http.service2
```

The function `aliasByNode` accepts a variable number of arguments, with the first being the query and the second being zero-based segments to use for the resulting name. The result is much easier to read.

Tracking Overall Incoming Requests

I've covered a lot of theory, so let's start sending some concrete data from your application and query against it. The first thing you will need to monitor in your service, assuming you respond to incoming HTTP requests, is the time it takes to reply to requests as well as the success or failure status of these requests. You'll probably want global statistics such as how many requests per second is the overall cluster serving and more granular statistics such as what is the average amount of time an endpoint takes to respond.

Duplicating this logic throughout your service's controllers would be messy and error-prone. Instead, you should abstract the calls using some sort of middleware, which will run regardless of which endpoint is getting executed. It's absolutely vital that you track every error being returned to the client (especially errors in the 5XX range), so be sure to generate some of these as part of your acceptance tests.

Overall Request Count and Timing

Tracking these stats can give you an overall picture of the health of the application. It will show you how many requests you're receiving and how long it takes to respond to a request. Listing 7-22 and Listing 7-23 show you how to track overall request counts and timings.

Listing 7-22. StatsD Calls

```
{SERVICE_NAME}.http.in.count
{SERVICE_NAME}.http.in.timing
```

Listing 7-23. Graphite Query

```
alias(stats.counters.{SERVICE_NAME}.http.in.count.count,
  "http_requests")
alias(stats.timing.{SERVICE_NAME}.http.in.timing.timing,
  "http_timing")
```

Overall Success and Failures

Listing 7-24 and Listing 7-25 will tell you what the success versus failure ratio of the application is. In the Display options of a Grafana graph, there is a section called Multiple Series. Enabling Stack and Percent will display these values as an overall ratio, which you can color red and green accordingly. In your application you'll want to classify status codes below 400 as success and above 400 as failure.

Listing 7-24. StatsD Calls

```
{SERVICE_NAME}.http.in.{success|failure}.count
```

Listing 7-25. Graphite Query

```
aliasByNode(stats.counters.{SERVICE_NAME}.http.in.
  {success|failure}.count.count, 6)
```

Overall Ratio of Status Codes

Listing 7-26 and Listing 7-27 are similar to the success and failure messages earlier but are much more granular. Depending on the observed spikes in status codes, you can tell whether many unauthenticated users hit an endpoint, whether a client started asking for an endpoint that doesn't exist, or whether a hacker is experimenting and generating many 400s.

Listing 7-26. StatsD Calls

```
{SERVICE_NAME}.http.in.status.{STATUS_CODE}.count
```

Listing 7-27. Graphite Query

```
aliasByNode(stats.counters.{SERVICE_NAME}.http.in
  .status.*.count.count, 6)
```

Per-Endpoint Count and Timing

Listing 7-28 and Listing 7-29 are useful for tracking how frequently used an endpoint is and which endpoints could use a boost in efficiency. If an endpoint is both slow and popular, it makes a great candidate to tackle during the next sprint. If some endpoints aren't used at all, then consider deprecating them.

Note that StatsD doesn't allow forward slashes, so if you plan on using the path to represent the endpoint, then slashes will need to be replaced with a different character such as an underscore.

Listing 7-28. StatsD Calls

```
{SERVICE_NAME}.http.in.endpoint.{ENDPOINT}.count
{SERVICE_NAME}.http.in.endpoint.{ENDPOINT}.timing
```

Listing 7-29. Graphite Query

```
aliasByNode(stats.counters.{SERVICE_NAME}.http.in
  .endpoint.*.count.count,  6,  8)
aliasByNode(stats.timing.{SERVICE_NAME}.http.in
  .endpoint.*.count.timing, 6, 8)
```

Tracking Outbound Requests

Your service should keep stats on every service it consumes. Any one of them could be detrimental to the health of your service either by bringing instability or by slowing down overall response time. By keeping stats, you can discern at a glance who is at fault.

> **Collaboration Tip**: You may be noticing there's a duplication of data here. If every service tracks the inbound and outbound request time, service A will know how long service B takes to respond, and service B will know how long itself takes to respond. This duplication is OK and can help find issues with network latency if the two systems report disparate numbers.

Much like with inbound HTTP requests, you'll keep track of the number of times you make outbound requests, which services you make requests to, the amount of time the services take to respond, and their status codes. One notable difference is that you'll also keep track of different low-level networking errors; these will help you debug situations where you aren't able to communicate with the remote service.

Tracking Timing

With each new deployment of a service comes a new opportunity for a developer to implement a slow nested loop. Keeping track of service timing will let you know who is to blame when the boss is standing behind you asking why everything is slow. Listing 7-30 and Listing 7-31 are examples of how you can do just that.

Listing 7-30. StatsD Calls

```
{SERVICE_NAME}.http.out.{REMOTE_NAME}.timing
```

Listing 7-31. Graphite Query

```
aliasByNode(stats.timing.{SERVICE_NAME}.http.out.*
  .timing.timing, 5)
```

Tracking Status Codes

Tracking outbound status codes is a great way to know whether everything is 2XX and happy, 4XX and you've broken something, or 5XX and they've broken something. You can achieve this using Listing 7-32 and Listing 7-33. If a server is unreachable and therefore no status code has been received, then default to 521 Service Unreachable.

143

Listing 7-32. StatsD Calls

```
{SERVICE_NAME}.http.out.status.{REMOTE_NAME}.count
```

Listing 7-33. Graphite Query

```
aliasByNode(stats.counters.{SERVICE_NAME}.http.out
  .status.*.count.count,  6)
```

Tracking Network Errors

Tracking network errors, like you do with Listing 7-34 and Listing 7-35, can give you insight into why connections to a remote server can fail (assuming your request library can surface such error codes). The names of the errors can be a little cryptic, but here's a quick guide to the codes and what they usually mean:

- ENETUNREACH (network is unreachable): Unable to talk to the network
- ECONNABORTED (software caused connection abort): Usually triggered by application code
- ECONNRESET (connection reset by peer): Host kills connection after it was established
- ETIMEDOUT (connection timed out): Host took too long to reply
- ECONNREFUSED (connection refused): Host is up but not listening on the port
- EHOSTUNREACH (no route to host): Unable to look up host via the Domain Name System (DNS)

Listing 7-34. StatsD Calls

```
{SERVICE_NAME}.http.out.error.{REMOTE_NAME}
  .{ERROR_CODE}.count
```

Listing 7-35. Graphite Query

```
aliasByNode(stats.counters.{SERVICE_NAME}.http.out
  .error.*.*.count.count, 6, 7)
```

Tracking Cache Lookups

When performance is vital to your service, you can't rely on the services you consume to also be performant. In these cases, it's good to cache data. Consider adding a caching layer in your service and enabling it for the slowest and least dependable services first. A highly configurable cache where expiration can be set on a per-resource-type basis is desirable.

Enabling caching is nice, but what's even nicer is knowing how frequently the cache is used (a cache hit) and how frequently it isn't and you need to contact an upstream service (cache miss). If a cache has an extremely high cache miss rate, it may mean that your cache key generation isn't that good or that the resource isn't worth caching at all. Listing 7-36 and Listing 7-37 show you a way you can track cache hits and misses.

Listing 7-36. StatsD Calls

```
{SERVICE_NAME}.cache.hit.{REMOTE_NAME}.count
{SERVICE_NAME}.cache.miss.{REMOTE_NAME}.count
```

Listing 7-37. Graphite Query

```
aliasByNode(stats.counters.{SERVICE_NAME}.cache
  .{hit|miss}.*.count.count, 4, 5)
```

Track Everything

Any asynchronous tasks you perform are also worthy of keeping analytics of. For example, if you're performing any kind of manual garbage collection tasks, keep track of the amount of time they take and when they occur. If you're purging records on a set schedule, then track how many records are being deleted. If you're building an index of recently modified resources from a provider, keep track of how many new items have appeared.

Databases are another great component to keep track of. Come up with a name for each query your application generates and keep track of the amount of time they take to complete. Maybe even count the number of times each query is made; perhaps you'll find edge cases where several queries are made in serial when a single query should be used instead.

Serialization of data can be expensive as well, especially in services that generate large JSON or XML payloads; all that string concatenation can really add up. This one might be harder to track depending on the HTTP framework you're using. If it's difficult, consider manually serializing the string and tracking the time it takes to do so before delivering that string to the consumer.

Once you've added enough tracking to your application, you can get a feel for how much time each operation takes. This will give you some great insight into where your service spends time and what needs to be made more efficient.

Alerting

You can do your absolute best to build stable software, but at the end of the day we're all human. There will be runtime errors. There will be network hiccups you're not accounting for. There will be race conditions. There will be a lack of disk space.

When these unanticipated errors start happening in production, you need a way to find out about them. Perhaps a few 5XX errors here and there isn't a big deal, but once you reach a certain threshold of failing requests, you'll want to sprint to action.

One naive approach is to have an application e-mail you when failures occur. But what do you do when you're at home sleeping? Getting a phone call may be what it takes to get you to wake up and ensure your service is contributing to the company's bottom line.

When sending alerts, you typically want to dispatch them based on who is on a certain team. Teams should be empowered to write their own alerts in a way that adhere to the service level agreement (SLA) requirements the organization has provided.

Normally you don't need to make the entire team aware of a problem (especially during off-hours), so you first send the alert to a single person. The person who should receive the alert at a certain period of time is considered on-call; this person is being chosen in a round-robin style (or following some sort of schedule). When a person is alerted, you typically refer to this as being *paged*. If a person is unable to respond to the page or if the page needs to go up the chain, you refer to this as *escalation*.

When Not to Alert

Despite how excited you are at the prospect of getting woken up at 4 a.m. on a Saturday, let's first look at some situations unworthy of an alert. The general rule of thumb is that if something isn't preventing customers from using your product and giving you money, then a situation isn't worthy of a page. There are no hard-and-fast rules, though; you'll have to figure out what works best for your team and your organization as a whole. Here are a few examples to think about:

- *Server instance crash*: A single instance of a server crashing probably isn't worth a page. Since you're being a good microservice practitioner and are running many instances in parallel, this crashing service might have affected only a single request. A single user might be seeing an error screen, can refresh the page, and can see a successful screen loaded by a different instance. Of course, if many services are failing, this becomes an issue worthy of paging.

- *Memory leak*: Memory leaks are another thing that sucks but also another thing that can wait until the morning for a fix. When services are leaking memory, it usually takes at least a few hours of debugging before a patch can be made. Memory leaks can also be slow, taking weeks to leak, or fast, taking hours. If you have your environment set up to decommission an instance once it hits a memory threshold, the problem will (temporarily) fix itself (such as a container scheduler killing the process). Of course, if processes are running out of memory in a matter of minutes and dying left and right, this should trigger a page.

- *Service is slow*: If a service is slower but still usable, it may not be worthy of a page. Sometimes these are easy to fix such as a server being CPU bound. Other times they will be more difficult like if a cache systematically expires in the evening and becomes cold at night.

- *Spike in the 400s*: What could it mean if your application normally serves 100 requests per minute with 2XX responses and suddenly gains 50 requests per minute with 4XX errors and the usual amount of 2XX successes? Considering the normal healthy traffic has stayed the same, these may be a search engine or a web scraper generating bad requests. If your service is available only internally, it could mean someone just started an erroneous server. If you get a spike in overall traffic and the success rate diminishes, this means your usual traffic is starting to fail.

Error Thresholds

Coming up with error thresholds can be an interesting process. One thing to consider is that the raw number of errors isn't a good indicator of the severity but rather the percentage of overall requests that are failing (or even the *change* in the rate of failures).

Let's consider the situation of an e-commerce web site. This site gets 1,000 requests per minute during typical peak hours during the week. If the error rate exceeds a threshold, perhaps 20 errors per minute over 5 minutes, you would consider this a page-worthy situation.

The site of course receives much less traffic at night. Perhaps it receives ten requests per minute around midnight. At this rate, it might only be worth paging if the error level exceeds one request per minute for five minutes.

Once Black Friday comes, the site will be hit with a massive flood of traffic and jumps up to 100,000 requests per minute. However, during this period the organization might be on "red alert." Instead of scaling the allowable error rate by two orders of magnitude to match the traffic, you might scale it up by only one, so an error rate of 200 requests per minute may trigger a page.

When first implementing an error-paging system, be prepared to change the thresholds many times and again when the next holiday happens. Also, apologizing in advance to your teammates isn't a bad idea as chances are you won't get it perfect your first try.

Having Someone Else Respond

Some organizations implement a concept called a network operations center (NOC). These are groups of people not on the teams building applications and are the first line of defense for fixing issues.

Consider making use of a NOC if your team is able to document common situations that can trigger alerts, including how to spot the problem and how to tell what the right team to escalate the issue to is. For example, if you keep analytics of upstream services and one of them is producing 5XX, you should document that the NOC should escalate the issue to the team causing the errors.

You would also want to document other things such as how to scale your services to more instances, how to kill a service that is misbehaving, and if all else fails how to get the page into the hands of the developer who caused the bug.

External Tools (Software as a Service)

The very nature of alerting is that you want to let someone know when a service in your organization is not healthy. When these situations happen, it could mean that not just one service is bad but possibly a whole slew of them. Even worse is when something catastrophic has happened like physical hardware dying, database corruption, DNS issues, or even major network issues are happening.

Who watches the watchmen?

—Juvenal, Satires

In those situations, it would be silly to think that an alerting tool you are running in-house would be capable of sending an alert! So, while most of this book has concentrated on open source tools (and I will cover open source alerting tools as well), there will be a larger emphasis in this chapter on third-party software as a service (SaaS) solutions (which usually means paid).

As each of the tools in this section specializes in something a little different, it's not unheard of for larger organizations to combine tools.

PagerDuty

PagerDuty [69] is probably the most popular tool for incident management. It offers an API (and there are plenty of clients available) for creating incidents, triggering pages, acknowledging incidents, and finally resolving incidents. Alerts can be sent via e-mail, text messages, phone calls, and any combination of these. Alerts can be sent to individuals and entire teams and can automatically escalate up each level until acknowledgment happens.

Pingdom

Pingdom [70] is a tool for making external requests to URLs at regular intervals. Requests are made from all over the world and can be used to spot DNS issues from different locations. While Pingdom is technically more of a monitoring tool, it does offer the ability to trigger alerts.

Nagios

Nagios [71] is probably the most hard-core tool for monitoring the health of applications. It can check how well your application is communicating with database tools such as Redis, MongoDB, MySQL, and PostgreSQL. It can check CPU and memory usage, disk usage, network bandwidth usage, and so on. It also has the ability to alert developers when any of these checks fail.

Internal Tools (Self-Hosted)

If you do choose to use a self-hosted tool for alerting, you need to be aware of a few caveats. If you host it on an internal server and your other servers are internal, you should have connections to at least two ISPs in case one goes down. If you don't host these internally, you should use a different hosting service company. Redundancies are vital.

Grafana 4.0

As of Grafana 4.0 [72] the ability to alert is now built in. This has a number of advantages versus other tools. If you are already logging your service analytics using StatsD and reading it with Grafana, the data is already there waiting for you! Another advantage is the ability to set thresholds visually using a graph of historical data, as seen in Figure 7-3. You can write queries against data and drag and drop the threshold.

When you'd like Grafana to send a notification, you can configure it to send one via Slack, PagerDuty, e-mail, or a "web hook," which allows you to integrate it with other services.

The limitation of this is that other pieces of information that aren't tracked via Grafana can't be used to trigger the alert (e.g., error logs displayed in Kibana). This means you'll either want to track more analytics using Grafana or use multiple systems for configuring alerting.

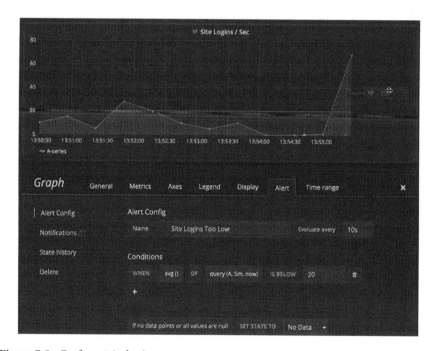

Figure 7-3. *Grafana 4.0 alerting*

Sensu

Sensu [73] is capable of doing many different types of monitoring. Essentially anything that can be represented as a shell script (cURL to request a URL, $ df -h to check disk space, CPU/memory usage) and return an exit status can be used for monitoring. It can be configured to talk to many alerting tools such as e-mail, PagerDuty, and chat apps. Sensu can be used as a central place to aggregate your checks (query Grafana, Kibana, etc.) before making the decision to trigger an alert.

CHAPTER 8

Documentation

Writing documentation is vital to the success of a service. If consumers don't know how to use your service, they won't use it. This is applicable to both services available to the public and those used only within an organization.

Good Documentation Principles

Make your documentation available to the public and search engines. Keeping documentation hidden behind a login prompt will have a few detriments. Developers won't be able to find documentation using a search engine, developers will be annoyed when they have to log in and navigate to the docs again, and potential developers won't know the capabilities of your application programming interface (API) before deciding whether they should sign up.

Automatic documentation generators can be useful as long as you make sure you're cleaning up the output and making it presentable. Generated docs can be useful with libraries where code connects directly to it or even Remote Procedure Call (RPC)–style APIs where the code and API are closely connected. However, automatically generated documentation can often leave much to be desired regarding quality and navigability, but it really depends on the tool.

For external, single-host APIs, do not truncate example resource request and response bodies; just show the whole thing. Even specify which Hypertext Transfer Protocol (HTTP) headers the consumer should expect to see. Make use of a syntax highlighter in your documentation because color-highlighted JavaScript Object Notation (JSON) is much easier to parse with human eyes.

Document the expected response codes and possible error messages for each endpoint and what could have gone wrong to cause those errors to happen. Dedicate a place where anticipated in-body error codes can be looked up as well.

Make sure your documentation can be printed. Cascading Style Sheets (CSS) is a powerful thing; don't be afraid to hide that sidebar when the docs are printed. Even if nobody prints a physical copy, you'd be surprised at how many developers like to export a PDF for offline reading.

Documentation can be either split into many different web pages or kept on one long page. If you are keeping documentation on one long page, be sure to break it up into sections with anchor tags and provide a table of contents so that developers can link to parts and share links with others. Long documentation can be hard to browse, and search engine results won't always link to the proper section of the document (this issue plagues the Lodash JavaScript documentation).

© Thomas Hunter II 2017
T. Hunter II, *Advanced Microservices*, DOI 10.1007/978-1-4842-2887-6_8

Convenience of Developer Testing

Providing convenient tools will allow developers to quickly test service interaction without having to paste sample code into their own applications. This allows them to get familiar with your API much quicker.

Web-Based Developer Console

A web-based developer console like the one in Figure 8-1 will allow developers to test API commands without ever leaving the documentation web site.

Figure 8-1. *Example API console*

You may already need a web site where third-party developers can register their applications, get authentication credentials, read documentation, and so on. This is a great place to put an API console.

Ensure the developer console is easy and efficient. Perhaps even provide them with a default user account that resets every hour using a cron job. Maybe by clicking a single button in their application listing, the three-legged authentication (3LA) credentials are automatically applied, and the developer can begin making service calls on behalf of their application immediately.

If possible, allow URL parameters to configure the developer console form. This way, a developer could click a link describing an API endpoint in the documentation and immediately be taken to the console where the endpoint is executed.

Providing cURL Commands

Services such as Mailgun, Stripe and even GitHub provide sample cURL commands. When doing two-legged authentication (2LA), the sample queries are easy to execute (3LA is often more difficult because of the required steps beforehand).

While cURL is available for Windows, if your service is primarily consumed by developers using Microsoft technologies, providing example cURL commands may not be as beneficial because many of these developers would not have cURL or find it helpful.

Listing 8-1 shows the example cURL command displayed on the Mailgun home page [74]. The provided API key is even functional, so by pasting this command into a terminal, you can instantly make a real API call!

Listing 8-1. Example Mailgun Home Page cURL Command

```
$ curl -s --user 'api:key-3ax6xnjp29jd6fds4gc373sgvjxteolo' \
  https://api.mailgun.net/v2/samples.mailgun.org/messages \
  -F from='Excited User <excited@samples.mailgun.org>' \
  -F to='devs@mailgun.net' \
  -F subject='Hello' \
  -F text='Testing some Mailgun awesomeness!'
```

Discovering Documentation

If your service represents an API that is available to the public, you should make your documentation easy to find. Unless your API is encumbered with nondisclosure agreements (NDAs), you should let it be indexable by search engines and easy to navigate to. Even if it does contain a lot of proprietary information, consider building a "Googleable" page with links to whatever authentication/sign-up page is required to get access to the docs.

If your service is entirely internal, you should still make the documentation easy to discover. Developers are a lazy bunch. They may or may not bookmark your documentation, and every time they forget how to find it, you don't want them coming to you with questions. If your company has an internal portal or wiki, you should host the documentation there. Or if your developers use a shared code repository (such as GitHub Enterprise), consider putting your documentation inside the repo's README (GitHub repos are easy to search and usually the first place an engineer will look).

If documentation for a service is hard to find, then developers won't know it exists and there's a risk that other people will re-create the same service.

Redundancy with links to documentation isn't a bad idea either. If you do keep docs in a wiki, then have your version control README link to the docs. Have your project chat room topic link to the docs. When you send e-mails to the organization discussing new features within a service, you guessed it, provide links to the docs. Eventually people will start bookmarking them.

Do your best to remove the barrier between developers and the knowledge they need to contribute to the organization.

Documentation Generators

Writing documentation manually can be tedious and error-prone. If documentation exists "far away" from the codebase it is documenting, the odds of documentation getting out-of-date is higher. Incorrect documentation is worse than no documentation. For these reasons, using documentation generation tools that extract information from the codebase will likely be more up-to-date.

Swagger

Swagger [75] is an open source suite of tools for dealing with API design. An important part of this suite is something called the Swagger specification. This allows you to describe an API. Listing 8-2 shows an example specification for a side project of mine.

Listing 8-2. Example Swagger Schema

```
---
swagger: '2.0'
info:
  version: 0.2.0
  title: Radar Server
  description: Example Interaction with the Radar Server
schemes:
  - https
host: api.radar.chat
basePath: /v1
paths:
  /channels/{channel_name}:
    parameters:
      - name: channel_name
        in: path
        description: Channel Name
        type: string
        required: true
    get:
      responses:
        200:
          description: Channel Information
        404:
          description: Channel not Found
```

The info section describes the overall API by giving it a name and description and a version.

The host, basePath, and schemes fields are used for defining the URL for the API.

The paths section is where you start describing the individual endpoints and methods allowed by your API.

In this example, I'm specifying only a single endpoint for getting information about a channel resource. It accepts a single parameter called channel_name, which is a URL segment. Parameters for other types of inputs can be described as well such as query parameters and form data.

Using this tool, you can also document the different response codes along with the meaning of each one.

These specification files can be used to generate documentation. They can be created using a normal text editor or with the Swagger editor, which is essentially a read-evaluate-print loop (REPL) allowing code to be modified and an interactive user interface (UI) generated at the same time. Figure 8-2 shows an example of this editor.

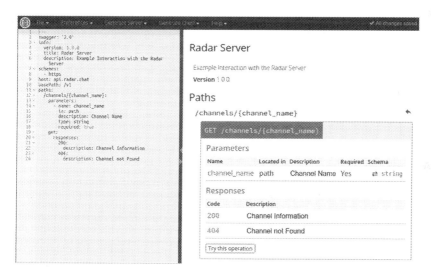

Figure 8-2. *Swagger editor*

Once you've generated a Swagger specification file, it can be converted into interactive web documentation that can be hosted as your API's documentation.

CHAPTER 9

Collaboration

You've undoubtedly noticed all of the Collaboration Tips mentioned throughout this book. The reason these have been so prevalent is because collaborating with members of other teams is important in the land of microservices.

The Importance of Collaboration

When an organization adopts microservices, you'll find a natural tendency for particular teams to own particular services. These services will begin to rely on one another, with service A relying on data from service B, service B relying on data from service C, D, and E, and so on.

Of course, as these dependency chains are introduced and the complexity of the overall organization increases, teams will start to depend on other teams to implement more features, provide more data, become more reliable, return data quicker, and so on. Communication between different teams becomes more and more important.

Your team will have deadlines to implement new features, which will require new features in upstream services, and time management comes into play in a much more complex way than if a single team were working on all aspects.

This chapter is all about how to effectively communicate with other teams, whether it be reproducing bugs, preventing reinvention of the wheel, or even lending a hand to help get required features implemented quicker.

Common Debugging Tools

It's important as a microservice-practicing organization to standardize on a few different tools for debugging communication between services. Of course, the tools mentioned in the preface of this book are the ones that I'm going to elaborate upon now.

cURL and jq

cURL [76] and jq [77] are amazing tools for a few reasons. They're entirely cross-platform, being available for macOS, Linux, and even Windows. They are both command-line tools that allow the piping of data from one to the other. Data piped in this manner can then be easily written to a filesystem or even piped back into cURL and sent off to another service!

© Thomas Hunter II 2017
T. Hunter II, *Advanced Microservices*, DOI 10.1007/978-1-4842-2887-6_9

Both of these tools can be a little off-putting to a novice, however. jq has its own powerful syntax for querying and manipulating JavaScript Object Notation (JSON) data. cURL has a myriad of flags that may need to be toggled depending on the quirks of the service it's communicating with.

Expect developers to have and be familiar with cURL and jq, but when it comes to nondeveloper roles, a tool with a graphical user interface (GUI) may be more appropriate.

cURL: Viewing Response Headers

The -i flag can be used to request that HTTP response headers be displayed before the body content, as shown in Listing 9-1. This is useful for debugging headers, as shown in Listing 9-2.

Listing 9-1. Displaying Response Headers with cURL

```
$ curl -i "https://api.github.com/repos/\
  tlhunter/node-grille/issues"
```

Listing 9-2. Response Headers in cURL Output

```
Server: GitHub.com
Date: Mon, 02 Jan 2017 02:19:57 GMT
Content-Type: application/json; charset=utf-8
Content-Length: 39780
Status: 200 OK
X-RateLimit-Limit: 60
X-RateLimit-Remaining: 55
X-RateLimit-Reset: 1483326978

[ { ...JSON BODY... } ]
```

cURL: Method and Request Headers

You have a few flags at your disposal for setting various request headers, not to mention specifying the all-important HTTP method. You can see these flags in use in Listing 9-3.

The -X <method> flag is used to specify the method you want to use.

The -H "<header: value>" flag is used to describe header pairs. They are specified using the full value of what would appear on a header line.

The -d <body> flag allows you to specify the content of the request body.

The last argument is the URL you want to request. To be safe, I recommend always wrapping it in double quotes; otherwise, you may run into weird shell escaping issues.

Listing 9-3. Specifying Method and Headers with cURL

```
$ curl -X POST \
    -H "Content-Type: application/json" \
    -H "Authorization: Basic MToxejFSUlRXUzFoV2c" \
    -d '{
        "name": "very-cool-channel",
        "listable": true
}' "https://api.radar.chat/v1/channels"
```

jq: Piping to jq

To get data to output from cURL and input into jq (or to output and input between any two commands), you can use the pipe operator (|). In its most basic form, jq can simply be used to provide syntax highlighting and whitespace readability.

You can see this happen with Listing 9-4, ,which uses the most basic jq operator, a humble period (.); this basically means to return what it receives. The output has whitespace and syntax highlighting applied, as shown in Listing 9-5.

Listing 9-4. Piping JSON into jq

```
$ echo '{"x": [1,2,3]}' | jq "."
```

Listing 9-5. JSON Formatting with jq

```
{
  "x": [
    1,
    2,
    3
  ]
}
```

Step 1: View Parsed Data

Ultimately what this section will show you is how to do the following: take an array of all issues tied to a particular GitHub repository; break them down into individual JSON objects; extract the title, state, url, and person attributes; and then combine them back into a valid JSON array.

The first thing you'll do is look at the output from the GitHub repository issues endpoint, as shown in Listing 9-6.

Listing 9-6. Piping All JSON to jq

```
$ curl "https://api.github.com/repos/tlhunter/\
node-grille/issues" | jq "."
```

This gives you the array of objects shown in Listing 9-7.

Listing 9-7. Complex List of Issues

```
[
  {
    "body": "blah blah blah",
    "closed_at": null,
    "updated_at": "2016-02-01T07:37:20Z",
    "created_at": "2016-02-01T07:37:20Z",
    "comments": 0,
    "number": 26,
    "id": 130284103,
    ...
    "user": { ... },
    "labels": [ ... ],
    "state": "open",
    "locked": false,
    "assignee": null,
    "assignees": [],
    "milestone": null
  },
  ...

]
```

Step 2: Separate Array Items

Before you can start interacting with the data provided in each of the issue objects, you need to remove them from being in an array. You can use the . [ ] construct, as shown in Listing 9-8, to break the array into individual items.

Listing 9-8. Separating Individual Array Items

```
$ curl "https://api.github.com/repos/tlhunter/\
node-grille/issues" | jq ".[]"
```

The data you receive from this call is no longer "valid JSON." You can instead think of it as something like a JSON stream. Each separate entry is valid JSON but not the whole thing. These results are now formatted like you see in Listing 9-9.

Listing 9-9. Individual Objects

```
{
  "id": 130284103,
  ...
},
```

```
{
  "id": 122875473,
  ...
}
```

Step 3: Extract Object Data

Now that you have individual objects, you can start to do work with them. Much like the pipe operator that you have in your shell, jq also gives you a pipe operator that works much the same way.

Here you are going to pipe each one of the previous objects into a new object ({}). This object will pull out properties of the object being passed into it. The names of properties you want to extract are separated by commas.

If you use simple names, shown in Listing 9-10 as state and url, the query will simply copy properties with the same name from the source to the new object. For more complex usage, you can use key/value pairs. In this example, title is pulled out by the longer syntax using title: .title. You can also grab more deeply nested properties using dot notation, as in person: .user.login.

Listing 9-10. Extracting Object Properties

```
$ curl "https://api.github.com/repos/tlhunter/\
node-grille/issues" | jq ".[] | {state, url, \
title: .title, person: .user.login}"
```

Listing 9-11 shows you that the output is still a "stream" of JSON data, though it is now much simpler.

Listing 9-11. Extracted Object Properties

```
{
  "person": "tlhunter",
  "url": "https://api.github.com/...",
  "state": "open",
  "title": "Parse XML in unit tests"
},
...
```

Step 4: Assemble Into Array

Finally, you can assemble everything back into a single valid JSON document by taking each of the individual objects and inserting them into an empty array. This is done by wrapping your operation in square brackets ([]), as shown in Listing 9-12.

Listing 9-12. Combining Objects into an Array

```
$ curl "https://api.github.com/repos/tlhunter/\
node-grille/issues" | jq "[.[] | {state, url, \
title: .title, person: .user.login}]"
```

Listing 9-13 assures you that the output is now an array of simplified issues containing only the data you want, as well as a valid JSON document.

Listing 9-13. Combined Array of Objects

```
[
  {
    "person": "tlhunter",
    "url": "https://api.github.com/...",
    "state": "open",
    "title": "Parse XML in unit tests"
  },
  ...
]
```

This is just a subset of the powerful jq query language. It's possible to do more advanced operations such as filter array items based on conditions applied to properties and perform arithmetic. I suggest you check out the jq documentation [77] and add it to your repertoire.

Postman

Postman is a great GUI-based tool for communicating with HTTP-based services (see Figure 9-1). Using the interface, you can define different environments (useful for setting hostnames), create collections (useful for describing a particular service), and define individual endpoints within a collection.

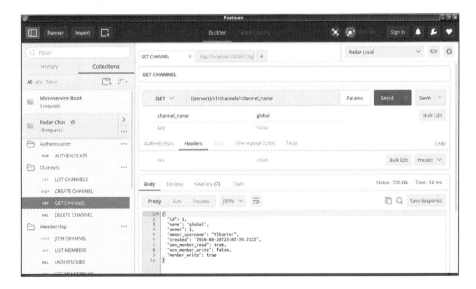

Figure 9-1. Postman, multiplatform

Another great feature with Postman is the ability to import and export collections and environments easily in the form of a single JSON file. These files can be checked into version control and easily shared among multiple teams. Imagine how convenient it would be if every team within your organization maintained a versioned list of endpoints so that other teams could quickly start making requests and examining data!

Postman also has a service where members of an organization can register accounts and share collections across a company.

Postman supports defining URL parameters using a special syntax. This allows you to change configuration options using GUI tools.

Environments

The Postman UI has a drop-down in the upper-right corner where you can select different environments. The environments your organization has chosen (such as Development, Staging, Production) can be entered as environments. Within each environment you can specify different key/value pairs. You could enter the following key/value pairs into Postman.

Production Environment

```
photos: https://photos.mysite.org
account: https://account.mysite.org
```

Staging Environment

```
photos: http://photos.staging.mysite.org
account: http://account.staging.mysite.org
```

Development Environment

```
photos: http://localhost:8080
account: http://localhost:8081
```

You can then use the drop-down to select between the different environments.

Example Addresses

When you input a URL in the address field, you can enter those same values except have them surrounded by double curly braces, such as {{photos}} shown in Listing 9-14. This will substitute the value with an environment-specific value, allowing you to quickly change environments without having to manually rewrite addresses.

Listing 9-14. Example Postman Addresses Using Environment Values

```
{{photos}}/v1/photos
{{account}}/v1/accounts/1234
```

Parameters

In the URL you can input placeholders as URL segments represented as simple strings prefixed with a colon (such as :user_id). These will be represented in the GUI to be easily changed.

Even query parameters will be listed in the UI. Figure 9-2 shows an example of this.

Figure 9-2. *Postman parameters*

Paw (Mac Shops)

If your organization is entirely made up of developers using macOS, it may be worth considering using Paw, a macOS native client (shown in Figure 9-3).

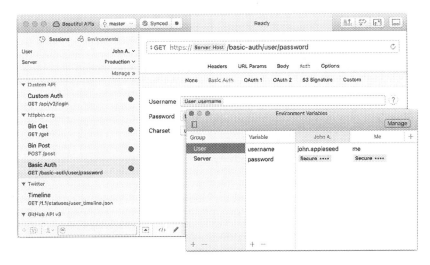

Figure 9-3. *Paw for macOS*

▓ **Note**   Keep in mind that requiring tools that work only on a subset of developer platforms will introduce unnecessary rigidity to your organization.

Fiddler 2 (Windows Shops)

If your organization is entirely made up of Windows developers, consider standardizing on the tool Fiddler 2 (shown in Figure 9-4).

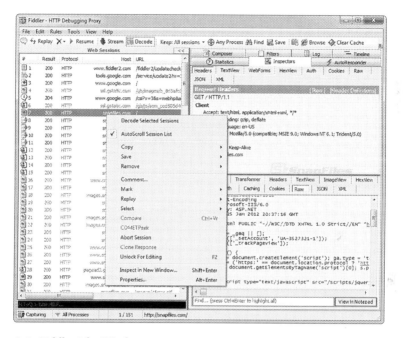

Figure 9-4. *Fiddler 2 for Windows*

Fiddler 2 isn't exactly in the same class as these other tools, but it has some robust features and is primarily used to act as an HTTP/HTTPS proxy. This allows you to debug traffic being sent over the wire (such as data sent from a client to a server). It does support the ability to generate and send requests.

Shared Modules

Your organization will naturally start to standardize on common patterns and services throughout different projects. For example, maybe all caching is performed using Redis, APIs exposed to the public use OAuth 2.0, most data ends up being stored in PostgreSQL, logs are aggregated using logstash, and analytics are collected via StatsD.

These common open source technologies will have client libraries available for almost any language you can throw at them, so finding the right library for the job probably won't be that hard to do.

However, the patterns you choose to implement these services in will likely be shared among different projects but may have to be re-implemented with each project. Looking at StatsD as an example, it's beneficial to log data in the same standard to make it easier to create dashboards as well as collect data that can be compared across all projects.

You could (and the first developer to implement probably will) implement these StatsD calls in your application code. These calls can be abstracted out and made into a module loaded by whatever web framework a project is using. This module can then be shared across teams, preventing future engineers from rebuilding the same application code.

If there is a common service used by many different services written in the same language, then each service will probably be writing redundant code to make HTTP requests, get data, parse it, and so on. Maybe there is a common user authentication service, and as a convention all services pass around the same X-User-ID HTTP header.

In cases like these, the owner of the user service should consider creating a common library to abstract the HTTP calls and expose a method that accepts an incoming HTTP request, parses out the user ID, passes it to the user service, and comes back with a populated user object. Other common features such as generating the password hash or handling session expiration can also be shared in this common module.

Logs are another great example. Assuming every service has its own name, all logs are sent to the same discoverable logging server, and each log should contain at a minimum a certain number of entries (timestamp, service name, user ID, request ID) and then create a shared module for generating and sending these logs! Once such a shared library has been created, it can be initialized with an application name and expose a method that accepts the user ID, request ID, and other dynamic information. The timestamp, service name, and discovering of the server are all abstracted away from the application developer.

Minimize Languages and Frameworks

Of course, sharing libraries works only under certain situations. If a library is written for .NET C# and a team comes along writing their service in Node.js, these shared libraries can no longer be shared. While it's healthy to use the right tool for the right job, there is much to be said about having a company choose a few core language/frameworks for building with.

A safe way to calculate the number of languages your organization should be using might look like Listing 9-15.

Listing 9-15. Back of the Napkin Calculation

```
max_languages = floor(sqrt(developers / 5))
```

With this equation I cobbled together, you may support 1 language at 5 employees, 2 at 20 employees, 3 at 45 employees, and so on. It is by no means a hard rule to live by, but it should help prevent your organization from spiraling into "polyglottic chaos."

Be Precise When Reporting Bugs

It doesn't matter where you work, those mean ol' project managers are going to be working you poor software engineers to the bone. Every team has its deadlines to reach, bugs to fix, features to implement, and spaghetti code to refactor (when no one is looking).

When you find that a service you depend on has some sort of bug or is sending you data in a hard-to-parse format, it is important to convey this bug to the other team in the clearest way possible. Forwarding an e-mail from a client with a screenshot of a glitch just isn't going to cut it!

You're going to need to share a reproducible query that the other team can execute and view themselves. When communicating this query (over e-mail, chat, an issue tracker, etc.), provide an example of the output you're getting as well as the output you're expecting. It could even be that you're the only affected project. Providing an easily reproduced bug so that the at-fault team doesn't need to is going to save that team time and increase the priority of your bug.

After investigating a bug and trying to point the blame at another team, you may even find that the bug is actually a problem either in how you're requesting data or in how you're handling the data once it comes back. If you do ask another team to invest time trying to reproduce a bug that is ultimately on your end, they will be less likely to accept bug reports from you in the future. You also risk looking like an idiot.

The burden of proving a bug is on the reporter.

Example of a Poorly Described Bug

The following is an example e-mail sent to the photos team that doesn't do a good job describing a bug:

> *"We're finding that the main user profile picture isn't loading for Chinese users. You can see this by using our shared Chinese test account test@ example.cn, logging into the Chinese web site example.cn, and visiting the profile page."*

While it is true that this does describe the bug and is reproducible, it does leave a bit to be desired. If your team owns the web site that displays the data, then the photo API team will not immediately know what request to their service is being generated. This will require extra work to either reply, dig through your codebase, or simply assume a certain endpoint is being used in a particular manner.

Another issue is that this bug only affects users of the Chinese web site. The bug itself doesn't specifically say that users of the American web site are not affected. This means a member of the Photos API team will need to make multiple requests to confirm when the bug happens.

Example of a Nicely Described Bug

The following is an example e-mail (with attached cURLs as shown in Listing 9-16) sent to the photos team that does a much better job describing a bug:

> *"The following query yields an invalid user profile picture (a null value) but only when asking for data on the Chinese profile page. It does work for profiles with any other language."*

Listing 9-16. cURLs and Their Outputs

```
$ curl \
  -X GET \
  -H "Accept-Language: zh-CN" \
  -H "Authorization: Basic abc123=" \
  -H "X-User-ID: 12345" \
  -H "Cache-Control: no-cache" \
  "http://api.example.cn/v1/user/12345"

{
  "email": "test@eample.cn",
  "image": null
}

$ curl \
  -X GET \
  -H "Accept-Language: en-US" \
  -H "Authorization: Basic def456=" \
  -H "X-User-ID: 456789" \
  -H "Cache-Control: no-cache" \
  "http://api.example.com/v1/user/456789"

{
  "email": "test@eample.com",
  "image": "http://im.example.com/456789.jpg"
}
```

This example is great because you've provided the photos API team with two queries and their outputs and have told them that the second output is what you desire in the first situation. They now know a situation where the code fails and a situation where it succeeds and can examine the logic that differentiates the two situations. The developer can copy and paste the two commands and see them happening exactly.

This example still isn't perfect. Can you spot the ambiguity? There are technically two properties separating the two queries from passing. The first query hits the Chinese API and requests the Chinese language, while the second hits the American API and requests the English language. If you were to swap the languages around, you might find that the error is specifically tied to either the Chinese language or the Chinese API, which would make debugging that much easier for the photos API team.

Generate cURLs Programmatically

Generating cURLs programmatically is probably one of the best solutions I've had for increasing debuggability for a service I maintain. One of my services consumed more than a dozen other services and was itself consumed by a few services.

Hunting down issues and reproducing them was difficult at first. I was logging outbound requests but in a naive way: a description of the request was being printed to the console by way of JSON. Whenever I would need to reproduce an issue, I would manually take this JSON data, hunt down the HTTP endpoint it would hit, look up the hostname and port in a discovery tool, and stich together a cURL statement by hand. How tedius!

Finally, I decided to simply generate a cURL statement programmatically. These would be generated only when the service was being run on a development machine. Since I was printing output to the console and it didn't need to be machine parseable, I would colorize the output to make it more readable. Whenever lines would exceed the character width of the terminal, I would break it down and use backslashes at the ends of lines (it's the shell syntax for multiline input, shown throughout this book).

The output would contain information such as the full URL with query parameters, the request method (e.g., `$ curl -X GET`), headers, and even POST bodies. It's important to ensure each part of the query is properly escaped so it can be immediately copied and pasted without any manual reformatting.

I'd also output the amount of time it took for a query to execute and the resulting status code of the response.

Once these changes were made, I could simply copy the cURL statement from the console and send it to a developer. This has turned a process that used to take several tedious minutes into an instant copy-and-paste task. I highly recommend taking this approach in your projects!

Patches Welcome

The most surefire way to get a blocking bug fixed is to contribute the necessary code change to the other team while adhering to all of their contribution guidelines. If someone reports a bug to you and you know it'll take a few hours to fix, then you're going to need to finish up what you're doing, reproduce the bug, get it working, write tests and meet code coverage guidelines, and so on. But imagine you see a pull request with the continuous integration checks all green, tests passing, no typos, and following the same filesystem structure used by the rest of the project. You won't be able to click Merge fast enough!

Coming up with a system to support this doesn't happen overnight. Your codebase will need to be discoverable by the other team. There will need to be ample documentation about how to check out the project, install the dependencies, compile, run tests and linters, and so on. It would be silly to tell someone that you are not going to accept their contribution because you've failed to explain the contribution requirements, wouldn't it?

Basically anything that you care about with regard to code quality needs to be automated. If you use Git for version control, you should implement a precommit hook to run the necessary checks. Configure your continuous integration project to run a superset of those checks and include heavier tests such as long-running integration tests.

Assuming you're using Git, then you can create a shell script and have it execute a command every time you perform a commit. This will fail future commits unless the script returns successfully (though the commit hook can be bypassed with a flag: `$ git commit --no-verify`). Listing 9-17 shows an example of doing this for a Node.js-based project.

Listing 9-17. Creating a Simple Git Pre-commit Hook

```
$ echo "npm test" > .git/hooks/pre-commit
$ chmod +x .git/hooks/pre-commit
```

If a contribution is made and is not accepted for any reason, you need to be precise when explaining why it will not be accepted. If any changes need to be made carefully, explain why. If the contribution needs to be discarded entirely, then tell them why in such a way that the contributor won't be afraid to make additional changes in the future.

References

[1] Joel Spolsky. Things You Should Never Do, Part I. https://www.joelonsoftware.com/2000/04/06/things-you-should-never-do-part-i/

[2] Wikipedia. List of TCP and UDP port numbers. https://en.wikipedia.org/wiki/List_of_TCP_and_UDP_port_numbers

[3] Corey Ballou. Why We Chose API First Development, 2013. http://blog.pop.co/post/67465239611/why-we-chose-api-first-development

[4] GitHub, Inc. GitHub v3 API, 2014. http://developer.github.com/v3

[5] Twitter, Inc. Twitter v1.1 API, 2014. https://dev.twitter.com/docs/api/1.1

[6] J. Gregorio, R. Fielding, M. Hadley, M. Nottingham, and D. Orchard. RFC 6570: URI Template, 2012. https://tools.ietf.org/html/rfc6570

[7] Wikipedia. Cross-origin resource sharing, 2012. https://en.wikipedia.org/wiki/Cross-origin_resource_sharing

[8] Jon Postel. Robustness principle, 1981. https://en.wikipedia.org/wiki/Robustness_principle

[9] J. Franks, P. Hallam-Baker, J. Hostetler, S. Lawrence, P. Leach, A. Luotonen, and L. Stewart. RFC 2617: HTTP Authentication: Basic and Digest Access Authentication, 1999. https://tools.ietf.org/html/rfc2617

[10] R. Fielding, J. Gettys, J. Mogul, H. Frystyk, L. Masinter, P. Leach, and T. Berners-Lee. RFC 2616: Hypertext Transfer Protocol – HTTP/1.1, 1999. https://tools.ietf.org/html/rfc2616

[11] International Organization for Standardization. ISO 8601: Data elements and interchange formats – Information interchange – Representation of dates and times, 1988. https://en.wikipedia.org/wiki/Iso8601

© Thomas Hunter II 2017
T. Hunter II, *Advanced Microservices*, DOI 10.1007/978-1-4842-2887-6

[12]   Stripe, Inc. Stripe API Reference, 2014.
https://stripe.com/docs/api

[13]   JSON Schema. Home page. http://json-schema.org

[14]   JSON API. Home page. http://jsonapi.org

[15]   Facebook. GraphQL. http://graphql.org/

[16]   Roy T. Fielding. Architectural Styles and the Design of
Network-based Software Architectures, Chapter 5. www.ics.
uci.edu/~fielding/pubs/dissertation/ rest_arch_style.htm

[17]   Wikipedia. Atom (standard): Example of an Atom
1.0 feed. https://en.wikipedia.org/wiki/
Atom_%28standard%29#Example_of_an_Atom_1.0_feed

[18]   The JSON-RPC Working Group. JSON-RPC 2.0 Specification.
www.jsonrpc.org/specification

[19]   Wikipedia. SOAP (Simple Object Access Protocol).
https://en.wikipedia.org/wiki/SOAP

[20]   Wikipedia. Unix philosophy. https://en.wikipedia.org/
wiki/Unix_philosophy

[21]   MessagePack. MessagePack: It's like JSON. but fast and small.
http://msgpack.org

[22]   Docker. Home page. https://www.docker.com/

[23]   Unionfs. Unionfs: A Stackable Unification File System.
http://unionfs.filesystems.org/

[24]   Docker. Dockerfile reference. https://docs.docker.com/
engine/reference/builder

[25]   Docker. Install Docker. https://docs.docker.com/engine/
installation/

[26]   Docker. Docker Hub. https://hub.docker.com/

[27]   Kubernetes. Production-Grade Container Orchestration.
http://kubernetes.io/

[28]   CoreOS. etcd. https://github.com/coreos/etcd

[29]   Kubernetes. Installing Kubernetes on Linux with kubeadm.
http://kubernetes.io/docs/getting-started-guides/kubeadm/

[30]   Wikipedia. Crontab. https://en.wikipedia.org/wiki/
Cron#Overview

[31]   Apache. Apache Mesos. http://mesos.apache.org/

[32]   Mesosphere. Marathon. https://mesosphere.github.io/
marathon/

[33]   Docker. Overview of Docker Compose.
       https://docs.docker.com/compose/overview/

[34]   Jenkins. Home page. https://jenkins.io/

[35]   Cloudbees. Jenkins Docker Pipeline Plugin.
       https://go.cloudbees.com/docs/cloudbees-documentation/
       cje-user-guide/index.html#docker-workflow

[36]   Jenkins. Using a Jenkinsfile. https://jenkins.io/doc/book/
       pipeline/jenkinsfile/

[37]   Jenkins. GitHub Pull Request Builder Plugin. https://wiki.
       jenkins-ci.org/display/JENKINS/GitHub+pull+request+b
       uilder+plugin

[38]   Travis CI. Home page. https://travis-ci.org

[39]   JetBrains. TeamCity. https://www.jetbrains.com/teamcity/

[40]   CircleCI. Home page. https://circleci.com/

[41]   Thomas Hunter II. 100 line Service Discovery example.
       https://github.com/tlhunter/node-discovery

[42]   HashiCorp. Consul. https://www.consul.io/

[43]   Nginx. Home page. https://www.nginx.com/

[44]   HAProxy. Home page. www.haproxy.org/

[45]   HashiCorp. Consul Template. https://github.com/
       hashicorp/consul-template

[46]   Thomas Hunter II. Consul HAProxy Example.
       https://github.com/tlhunter/consul-haproxy-example

[47]   Apache. ZooKeeper. https://zooKeeper.apache.org/

[48]   Apache. Curator. http://curator.apache.org/

[49]   Netflix. Eureka. https://github.com/Netflix/eureka

[50]   PostgreSQL. Home page. https://www.postgresql.org/

[51]   Wikipedia. ACID. https://en.wikipedia.org/wiki/ACID

[52]   MongoDB, Inc. MongoDB. https://www.mongodb.com/

[53]   MongoDB, Inc. Query and Projection Operators. https://
       docs.mongodb.com/manual/reference/operator/query/

[54]   Redis. Home page. https://redis.io/

[55]   Redis. Redis configuration. https://redis.io/topics/config

[56]   Elastic. Elasticsearch. https://www.elastic.co/products/
       elasticsearch

[57]   Roy T. Fielding and Richard N. Taylor. *ACM Transactions on Internet Technology (TOIT)*, volume 2. ACM, University of California, Irvine, 2002. `www.ics.uci.edu/~taylor/documents/2002-REST-TOIT.pdf`

[58]   Ed. D. Hardt. RFC 6749: The OAuth 2.0 Authorization Framework, 2012. `https://tools.ietf.org/html/rfc6749`

[59]   Ed. E. Hammer-Lahav. RFC 5849: The OAuth 1.0 Protocol, 2010. `https://tools.ietf.org/html/rfc5849`

[60]   Coinbase. API Authentication, 2014. `https://coinbase.com/docs/api/authentication`

[61]   Elastic. Kibana. `https://www.elastic.co/products/kibana`

[62]   Elastic. Logstash. `https://www.elastic.co/products/logstash`

[63]   Apache. Lucene Query Parser Syntax. `https://lucene.apache.org/core/2_9_4/queryparsersyntax.html`

[64]   Grafana. Beautiful metric and analytic dashboards. `http://grafana.org`

[65]   Graphite. Make it easy to store and graph metrics. `https://graphiteapp.org`

[66]   StatsD. Daemon for easy but powerful stats aggregation. `https://github.com/etsy/statsd`

[67]   StatsD. StatsD Metric Types. `https://github.com/etsy/statsd/blob/master/docs/metric_types.md`

[68]   Graphite. Functions. `http://graphite.readthedocs.io/en/latest/functions.html`

[69]   PagerDuty. Home page. `https://www.pagerduty.com/`

[70]   Pingdom. Home page. `https://www.pingdom.com/product`

[71]   Nagios. Home page. `https://www.nagios.org/`

[72]   Grafana. Grafana 4.0 Beta Release Notes. `http://grafana.org/blog/2016/11/09/grafana-4.0-beta-release/`

[73]   Sensu. Home page. `https://sensuapp.org`

[74]   Mailgun, Inc. Home page, 2014. `www.mailgun.com`

[75]   Swagger. Home page. `http://swagger.io/`

[76]   cURL. Home page. `https://curl.haxx.se/`

[77]   jq. Home page. `https://stedolan.github.io/jq/`

Index

© Thomas Hunter II 2017
T. Hunter II, *Advanced Microservices*, DOI 10.1007/978-1-4842-2887-6

Get the eBook for only $5!

Why limit yourself?

With most of our titles available in both PDF and ePUB format, you can access your content wherever and however you wish—on your PC, phone, tablet, or reader.

Since you've purchased this print book, we are happy to offer you the eBook for just $5.

To learn more, go to http://www.apress.com/companion or contact support@apress.com.

Apress®

All Apress eBooks are subject to copyright. All rights are reserved by the Publisher, whether the whole or part of the material is concerned, specifically the rights of translation, reprinting, reuse of illustrations, recitation, broadcasting, reproduction on microfilms or in any other physical way, and transmission or information storage and retrieval, electronic adaptation, computer software, or by similar or dissimilar methodology now known or hereafter developed. Exempted from this legal reservation are brief excerpts in connection with reviews or scholarly analysis or material supplied specifically for the purpose of being entered and executed on a computer system, for exclusive use by the purchaser of the work. Duplication of this publication or parts thereof is permitted only under the provisions of the Copyright Law of the Publisher's location, in its current version, and permission for use must always be obtained from Springer. Permissions for use may be obtained through RightsLink at the Copyright Clearance Center. Violations are liable to prosecution under the respective Copyright Law.

Printed in the United States
By Bookmasters